D1258937

Serving God wholeheartedly

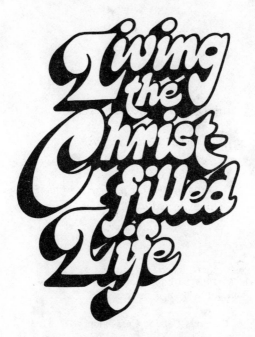

Living the Christ-filled Life

John E. Hunter

ZONDERVAN PUBLISHING HOUSE
OF THE ZONDERVAN CORPORATION
GRAND RAPIDS, MICHIGAN 49506

CONTENTS

Living the Christ-filled Life

CHAPTER 1

NO SPRING FOR A DEAD TREE

It has been my privilege to travel in many countries, to see much wonderful scenery, and to stand in awe at the amazing handiwork of God in creation. I have been impressed and challenged again and again, but nothing ever moves me so much as to be in the English countryside in the springtime.

I am always fascinated by the quiet emergence of the new life from the cold deadness of the fading winter. In every area of plant life, of bird and animal life, the countryside stirs itself and becomes gloriously involved in the miracle of springtime.

Against a new backdrop of tree scenery the tiny actors play their parts in God's annual masterpiece, accompanied by the sounds of newly-tuned songs.

Spring is a blessed and happy time for trees. Once more they can develop their full leafy personality. But this is not so for all trees—there is no spring for a dead tree!

When I lived in the country I would watch many a copse or rolling wood when the magic months came. I would see bare and empty trees emerging from the nakedness of winter, glowing green to change the whole countryside.

But, when I looked deeper into the woods, I would see trees that showed no response to increasing sunshine and the call of the new-time. They had no capacity to emerge because they were dead–and there is no spring for a dead tree!

So it is in the realm of the human heart. The God of creation is the God of redemption, and God's salvation begins with being born again—as Jesus said in John 3:3. Being born again is receiving a new quality of life. The first birth brings physical life and mental ability, but it also includes what Ephesians 2:1 calls being "dead in sins"—spiritually dead.

This is why Jesus said in John 10:10: "I am come that they might have life, and that they might have it more abundantly." His inclusive work was to bring spiritual life to the human spirit, on the basis of forgiveness of sins. Romans 8:16 says: "The Spirit himself beareth witness with our spirit, that we are the children of God." (ASV).

God's salvation is thus the springtime of the soul. There is a new quality of life at work within the human heart and life of the believer. The brown withered leaves of the old dead life fall off under the expulsive power of a new resurgence of the spiritual dynamic.

> Heaven above is softer blue,
> Earth around is sweeter green,
> Something lives in every hue
> Christless eyes have never seen.

But, remember, just as there is no spring for a dead tree—so there is no spiritual spring for the soul without this newness of Christ indwelling through His Holy Spirit.

You can care for a dead tree, prune it, fertilize it, transplant it—but you cannot bring spring to its empty deadness.

Likewise, you can bring new practices to the soul without Christ, involving education, new techniques of worship, even moving to a new church or denomination—but without the glorious experience of receiving Christ into the heart and life, the only result is a new type of deadness.

Yes, springtime is tremendous, but no tree is ever satisfied by springtime alone. The same resurgence of life that brings the spring goes on to bring the fullness of summer, and the complete satisfaction of a fruitful autumn. Only when the wheel has turned full circle is the tree satisfied. Then it can rest with the quiet assurance of 'mission accomplished.'

In just the same way, being born again is not, of itself, the aim of spiritual experience. This is but the springtime of the soul. For full satisfaction there must be the going on to summer and autumn. Just as in the case of the tree– the same life that brought the spring must bring the summer and the harvest.

This is where so many Christians miss the supreme glory of the outworking of the indwelling Christ. We come as sinners to the cross. We receive Christ into our hearts and lives. We are born again and move into the thrilling wonder of sins forgiven and a home in heaven. Then, we do one of two things. We settle down to enjoy our springtime, believing that spring is the final act. Or we set about organizing our own summer and producing our own autumn, under the mistaken impression that we are responsible for the results.

Trees do not operate that way and neither does God. The same life that brings the spring to the soul guarantees the harvest–and that Life is Christ indwelling us through His Holy Spirit.

The purpose of this book is to consider this whole process more thoroughly. We will consider how your springtime can go on to summer and then to a fruitful harvest. We will learn how, instead of displaying only a crop of leaves, the flowers of Christian character may be seen . . . to be followed by the fruits of Christian service. This will be, indeed . . . Living the Christ-filled life.

CHAPTER 2

JESUS CHRIST THE ONLY ANSWER

"Then Philip opened his mouth, and began at the same scripture, and preached unto him Jesus" (Acts 8:35).

In these days many people are trying to find God by varying methods, in different places, and by self-thought and beliefs. They are so accustomed to the ways of business, so used to the ways of the world around them, that they associate the Christian faith with a place, a personality, a plan, a program. Very often Christians and church members make the same mistake, that of judging spiritual truth by non-spiritual standards. They have no expanse of vision, they become so spiritually shortsighted that their effectiveness for God and their usefulness in His service are sadly limited. Only the word of God can give us the answer.

In Acts 8:26-29 we read of one who represents man at his very best. He is described as "of great authority" (Acts 8:27), in charge of the treasury department of Ethiopia. Chosen by Candace the Queen, and personally responsible to her, he must have been of the highest integrity for he had control of all her great treasure. Such a man would be of high birth, aristocratic upbringing, of excellent education and professional ability. Naturally he would be very rich and his riches would give him access to all that many men count dear. He must have been fairly young and strong because he had unusual experiences in travel, so rare in those days.

(It is worth pausing here to realize that the Lord Jesus lived His earthly life in an area of 100 miles by 60 miles.

10

Visualize 100 miles and that was the length of Christ's journeying.)

The man of Ethiopia was a great traveler by standards of the day. He appears to have had everything that could make a man happy, everything to satisfy the human heart—riches, responsibility, renown, royalty, and yet he wasn't satisfied. He was seeking peace with God, a complete satisfaction of his soul's hunger and desire.

We know what he was seeking by the kind of books he read. This is an important point to realize—the kind of books we read are a good guide to the kind of things we want! If I see you reading mathematics, physics and chemistry books I will know that you are probably studying eventually for an examination. I can guess your hobbies from the books you read—sport, photography, gardening, etc.

Show me your books and I will tell you your character. If I see you reading doubtful books which are sexy, debasing and sordid, I will know that is what you want—a cheap thrill, sin without symptoms! If you read nothing, you are nothing. If you read the Word of God you have the availability of God in your personality. The Ethiopian Eunuch was seeking peace and the answer to grief, sorrow, iniquity and sin, seeking something to meet the hunger of his heart.

There are many people today who are just as hungry for some similar form of satisfaction but they cannot put words to it. So many believe that enough wealth will bring real satisfaction. If only they have enough money to satisfy all their wants and desires then they will be really happy. The Ethiopian had everything, but this peace.

The fact, that riches cannot buy peace, is borne out by today's suicide rate. General statistics show that those who die by their own hands are not those struggling for satisfaction, but those who have made enough to meet all their wants and who then realize that "A man's life consisteth not in the abundance of the things which he possesseth" (Luke 12:15).

11

The Ethiopian, seeking this peace, journeyed to Jerusalem, the center of the religious world in that day. His round trip would be over 2,000 miles made in a chariot without springs, over roads without a surface, under conditions unfavorable to any human comfort. Such a journey was surely a proof of a man's sincerity. He came to Jerusalem to the glorious temple. He would see the most colorful religious services possible. He would hear the singing of the wonderfully trained choirs with the accompanying orchestras. He would move among the most religious people of his day. Everywhere was the opportunity to contact religion, and find the answer to the ache in his heart. But he left the place of religion wihout the peace of God. God's salvation is not in a place. You may find ritual and respectability and religion in a place, but not God's salvation.

Before he left he bought a copy of the book of the prophet Isaiah. Such a book or roll must have been very expensive, all handwritten on parchment. Here again the price he paid indicates the desire of his heart. As his chariot bumped on its homeward journey he tried to find peace with God in the passages he read, but he failed. It was a closed book to him and he hadn't the key to unlock the message. Thus he had come to the end of his resources. His wealth, high birth, great education, strength and youth, and governmental standing, had all failed to satisfy him. But now God steps in and takes over.

How rapidly events move when God steps in. Philip asks the one question: "Understandest thou what thou readest? (Acts 8:30), and when this great man admits his failure, then Philip starts and preaches from the same Scripture. Philip preached Jesus–a Person. Into the closed door of the Word of God Philip placed the blessed key which is Christ, and everything became plain. The full message of God's salvation in Christ was proclaimed, and the man believed. What a glorious end–he was baptized and went on his way rejoicing, and he never stopped rejoicing. He only heard one gospel message in all his life, but that was enough. All he needed was Jesus.

He went back to his homeland without a Bible, without a prayer book, hymnbook or chorus book. He had no church to help him, no minister or pastor to guide him, no religious publications to read, no correspondence courses to follow, no Christian fellowship to comfort and strengthen him, no follow-up work to keep him—nothing but the knowledge of Christ as his salvation. What an amazing thought, and yet it is challenging to see that history reports that when, in later years, Christian missionaries went to Ethiopia they found groups of people worshiping and rejoicing in the Lord Jesus Christ. The man's rejoicing was infectious; others caught it, and it never ceased.

The secret, of course, was in the message of Philip. Philip only had one text—Jesus Christ. He only had one sermon—Jesus Christ (Acts 8:5, 35). In this he was following the true apostolic tradition.

We read in Acts 5:42 concerning the apostles: "And daily in the temple, and in every house, they ceased not to teach and preach Jesus Christ." They had only one text and one sermon—God's salvation in a Person. Paul, in Acts 9:20, preached his first Christian message: "And straightway he preached Christ in the synagogues." In Acts 10:36, 43 Peter preaches the same message. Paul again in Acts 13:38 testifies: "Through this man is preached unto you the forgiveness of sins." Again in Acts 17:18, Paul preached unto the Athenians "Jesus." Just consider, they had no buildings, no plans, no committees, no programs, no organizations, but they did have *POWER*. It was said of them: "These that have turned the world upside down are come hither also" (Acts 17:6). What a complaint! The point was that all their preaching was related to the Person of Christ, not only His work but His Person. He Himself is God's full salvation.

Today many so called Christians have fallen into the mistake of approaching the spiritual along the lines of the earthly. We seek to reach men in their bitter need by our places (churches), our programs, our plans, our preparations, our peculiarities, our personalities. These things are good and useful in their proper places, but they have no power in themselves alone. They can characterize an organization but never an organism; an organism has *life,* which no organization has. Without the Person of Christ they are merely social, but when Christ is the only text–the meanest and simplest group becomes charged with the dynamic of God.

There is a famous painting called "The Presence." The artist has painted it as looking from the back of a church. Away at the other end a colorful religious ceremony is being enacted. The altar is bright with candles and crucifixes. The priest and choir are superbly robed and singing with majestic wonder. The congregation, rather small, is attracted to this scene as moths to a candle. But in the back seat, away from it all, a poor woman is bowed, the picture of abject sorrow and misery. Yet standing alongside the woman is the mystic figure of the Person of Christ, His hand laid on her bowed head. How powerful is the message of the painter. Religion can attract, but it cannot heal the brokenhearted.

The Roman Catholic faith centers around the place of Bethlehem. There is the greater, more effective, figure of the holy mother Mary and the tiny, weak, helpless Babe. All true to a point, but when this aspect is magnified the balance is destroyed and Christ only fits into the picture. Gone is the clean, wholesome fullness of His power. This wasn't the message of the early church warriors.

The evangelical Christian often counters this by concentrating on the place of Calvary, the place of the center cross, the place of the empty tomb. But this in turn, can limit the truth of God. Hymn writers have written poetically of the cross, "To the old rugged cross I will ever be true."

We know what is the true meaning they seek to convey, but not everyone does. God's salvation is not in a place. God's salvation is not only the work of Christ, but in the Person of Christ–He is God's salvation. Simeon's famous prayer was: "For mine eyes have seen thy salvation" (Luke 2:30). This is not a quibbling over words, but an essential aspect of a vital, dynamic faith. If my faith is fixed to a place it easily becomes sentimental, with a sense of respectable ineffectiveness. But Christ is alive! If He is my salvation, then from this springs all the endless excitement of a vivid, living experience of His life in me.

In John 5:39 Jesus said to very religious people: "Search the scriptures; for in them ye think ye have eternal life: and they are they which testify of me."

Jesus Christ is bigger than Bethlehem, greater than Calvary, and more precious even than His own precious Word. Thousands have tried to run their lives by His teachings, quoting or misquoting the Word of God as their guide, but there is no salvation in the Word of God. Some with a fanatical zeal appear almost to worship the Bible. Let us be careful; salvation is not in the Scriptures –Jesus said so!

"The letter killeth" (II Corinthians 3:6). It is possible to have an intimate knowledge of the Word of God and still be lost. It is possible to know the truths of God's Word and still be a hard, bitter, narrow-minded person without the joyous, powerful effectiveness of the Christ-centered life.

There is such a freshness in relating my salvation to a living Saviour. There is that extra something that triumphs over the weakness of suffering and the weariness of age. That fullness of salvation which keeps me living in the present tense of One who could say, "I am"–never "I was"; "I am"–never–"I will be." A present tense experience of victory, joy, worth-whileness, the absolute certainty in a Person. Remember it is "Jesus Christ the same yesterday, and to day, and for ever" (Hebrews 13:8). He is always and at all times the same. Churches have changed; denominations have passed away; doctrinal truths have risen and fallen in importance and emphasis, but always "He is the same."

"Lo, I am with you always" (Matthew 28:20). What a blessed promise from a blessed Person. If our faith is dependent on the Word of God only, how dangerous that can be.

Geoffrey Bull, an English missionary, was imprisoned

by the Chinese Communists for several years. He records in his book, *When Iron Gates Yield,* how he was imprisoned in a terrible dungeon. Then his Bible was taken away, but his faith triumphed because, "Notwithstanding the Lord stood with me and strengthened me" (II Timothy 4:17). He only had Christ. But Christ was the power who turned the world upside down in apostolic days, and it is Christ who today can make "iron gates yield." If Christ Himself is your full salvation you need nothing more. "Ye are complete in him" (Colossians 2:10). He is yours and you are His for all times and for all places and conditions.

Living in the light and truth of this fact is the everlasting answer to all testing and temptation, to all sorrow and suffering, even to defeat, and death itself: "Yea, though I walk through the valley of the shadow of death, I will fear no evil: for thou art with me" (Psalm 23:4).

CHAPTER 3

JESUS CHRIST, MY FULL SALVATION

"For if, when we were enemies, we were reconciled to God by the death of his Son, much more, being reconciled, we shall be saved by his life" (Romans 5:10).

We read in Romans 5:8: "God commendeth his love toward us, in that, while we were yet sinners, Christ died for us." Here we have clearly stated the truth that the death of Christ was for all sinners. Verse 9 adds this further word that we were: "justified by his blood." Our sins are forgiven, they are put away, they are gone.

Many Christians know only this aspect of God's salvation. They have been to Jesus and their sins have been forgiven; they are "saved." With this limited knowledge of God's salvation they then go out to "be Christians," and no one need be surprised if very soon they are living the same kind of life they were before. They will then say they have tried religion but it failed, or, as often happens, they will make another profession of salvation to get their sins forgiven again, and go out once more into a life of inevitable failure. It is good to see that there is more than having your sins forgiven. In fact, the first two words of Romans 5:9 are these–*"Much more. . . ."*

The whole of Romans 5:9 says: "Much more then, being now justified by His blood, we shall be saved from wrath through him." Here it is stated quite simply the fact that *we shall be saved*. Because my sins are put away by the blood of Christ then that which separated me from my God has been put away also, and "we have peace with God through our Lord Jesus Christ" (Romans 5:1). The

Biblical word for this is "being reconciled." We are reconciled to God—not God to us. We are the guilty ones; we have to be reconciled. Because we are reconciled, we shall be saved from wrath to come. There will be no Great White Throne for us, no eternal separation to a lost eternity. Instead we have a home in heaven.

Some people are not sure about their home in heaven, they have doubts about their future salvation. This is sad because they have no assurance. They miss the point that He *is* my salvation. My safety does not depend upon what I keep on doing, but upon what He is.

But most Christians know Christ died for their sins and they know they have peace with God. The load of sin is gone and a home in Heaven is sure. What happens now is perhaps the biggest tragedy in the Christian life. Having received a past and a future salvation they now set out to spend the present time fighting the fight of faith. They fight and struggle, they plot and plan, they worry and scheme, all with the best intentions of living the Christian life.

If their struggles entail suffering and hardship they accept it as part of the price they pay as they try to gain the victory day by day. They miss the Scripture message that there is more than having their sins forgiven and having a home in heaven.

The whole verse of Romans 5:10 says:

> For if, when we were enemies, we were reconciled to God by the death of his Son, much more, being reconciled, we shall be saved by his life.

Because we have been reconciled, we shall be saved by His life. Most people would say they were saved by His death, yet here it states *saved by His life*.

The unfortunate fact is that these words: "We shall be saved by His life" are a very poor and inadequate translation of the original Greek. A more comprehensive translation is that given in the Amplified Version: "We shall be daily delivered from sin's dominion by His resurrection life." That is the whole emphasis—daily delivered—a

18

glorious present tense experience. How complete is the whole sequence: Justified by His blood, reconciled by His death, and daily delivered by His life.

Matthew 1:21 says: "Thou shall call his name Jesus: for he shall save his people from their sins." And I Timothy 1:15 says "This is a faithful saying, and worthy of all acceptation, that Christ Jesus came into the world to save sinners; of whom I am chief." Thus, first of all, I must realize that if I come as a sinner, if I confess my sin and recognize my need and claim Jesus Christ as my Saviour, then I can know by faith, that my sins are gone.

I now recognize, according to our Scripture, that there is much more than forgiveness of sins. Because my sins have been dealt with, then I am reconciled to God, I have peace with God, and am assured of a home in heaven.

Having identified myself with Christ in His death I now go on to claim the present salvation that is mine through His indwelling life. How can His resurrection life give me a daily deliverance from sin's dominion? The Bible promises this, how can I make it mine?

First I must realize that when I became a Christian I was born again. I received a new LIFE, eternal life. This LIFE is Christ Himself. He said: "I am the way, the truth, and the life" (John 14:6). We read in Romans 6:23: "For the wages of sin is death; but the gift of God is eternal life through Jesus Christ our Lord."

I John 5:12 says: "He that hath the Son hath life; and he that hath not the Son of God hath not life." Jesus Christ lives in me in the power and person of His Holy Spirit. Romans 8:9 says: "If any man have not the Spirit of Christ, he is none of his."

I now have to realize that Christ lives in me to give me daily deliverance from sin's dominion. He is the present tense of our salvation. I must prove experimentally the truth of I John 4:4: "Greater is he that is in you, than he that is in the world." So often as Christians we accept the fact that Christ lives in us in a casual kind of way. The attitude we show is quite academic.

19

"Yes," we say, "Christ lives in us, the Holy Spirit lives in us—but what difference does it make?"

We accept the fact, but deny the consequences. To our own cost we push aside the possibility of a present-tense experience of God's salvation, because we are so busy living the Christian life in our own way.

We never learn by experience that we cannot gain the victory over sin. We always hope to meet the victory somehow by our own endeavors.

We believe that if we can only follow the right pattern, go to the right Church, or read the right book, then we can find the "super" experience. And all the time God has made full provision for our present salvation. Because we miss the daily deliverance, we miss the blessing of the next verse, Romans 5:11: "And not only so, but we also joy in God through our Lord Jesus Christ." We never have the fullness of joy because we have either fully occupied ourselves in the struggle to do the impossible, or resigned ourselves to something which is less than God's best for us.

For so many of us our biggest problem is the present. It *is* good to know my sins are forgiven, and very comforting to look forward to a home in Heaven, but many Christians are mainly interested with the actual present— its problems and its defeats. Most Christians are defeated at some point in their daily living.

"The lust of the flesh, and the lust of the eyes, and the pride of life" (I John 2:16) work daily havoc in the lives of God's children.

The vital truth of Christ living His life in me is the *only* answer to this problem.

Paul repeatedly used the phrase "Christ in me" or "In Christ." This has been called Paul's magnificent obsession, for he uses the phrase more than 170 times. Galatians 2:20 is a good example: "I am crucified with Christ: nevertheless I live; yet not I, but Christ liveth in me."

What a difference this sense of Christ's life in me ought to make in my daily living. The responsibility should roll

20

off my shoulders. As I commit my life to Him, I would become His responsibility completely, for He not only saves but He keeps. I would know victory in my personal life where once I only knew defeat. As the sin that tempted so successfully in days past returned to the attack, I could step back in simple faith and say "Blessed Lord, this thing is too big for me; I've always given in before, but, Lord, nothing is too great for You. Please meet this for me in Your strength."

Then I would know that victory would be inevitable.

I would also get a new standard of values. I would see that the priorities of the world's system need no longer be the priorities in my life. As I seek first the kingdom of God the other "things" in my life would take their proper place. I could dare to stand back from the mad rush of life around me and know the peace of God which passeth all understanding.

Jesus said in John 13:17: "If ye know these things, happy (or blessed) are ye if ye do them." How far is this truth working in your life? Is it only in your head? That will never bring peace and blessing. Dare you commit yourself and identify yourself with Christ so that He can take over the present tense of your daily life?

God is the author of every good and *perfect* gift, and thus God's salvation is perfect. The imperfections arise when we present a "shortened version," or limit the area of God's opportunity, either in tense or place.

Some years ago the Bishop of Durham, England, was Dr. Wescott. He was a real saint of God, one of the greatest scholars of his day, a real believer with a great sense of humor. One day he had to make a train journey, and, as English trains then had carriages containing separate compartments for six people only, he sought and found an empty compartment and settled down to read quietly.

Just as the train was moving away from the station, the carriage door was opened, and a young girl in Salvation Army uniform jumped in. After she had settled herself in her corner she realized that the only other person with her was, as indicated by his distinctive garb, a real live bishop. She hadn't long been converted, and was keen to win others for Christ. Therefore, when she saw a real live bishop, and realized that he would be her companion for at least another hour, she planned how she could lead him to Christ. She assumed that because he was a bishop, in her opinion, he couldn't be a real believer!

Presently she leaned across to the bishop, who was reading, and said very abruptly, "Excuse me, are you saved?"

This short, but unexpected question caught Dr. Wescott by surprise, and he said in his kindly way, "Pardon me, but what did you say?"

She immediately thought, "There, he doesn't even know what I'm talking about!" and so explained, "I simply asked if you were saved."

The bishop's face disappeared behind his book and his eyes twinkled merrily for a moment; then, leaning toward her he asked her, "Excuse me, my dear, but do you mean *sotheis* or *sezosmenos* or *sozomenos?*" The girl's face went blank, then puzzled, then startled. Finally she blurted out, "I don't know what you are talking about. I simply asked you—were you saved."

"Yes, my dear," replied Dr. Wescott, "I realized that, and I asked you which "saved" you mean. Did you mean "I was saved" or "I will be saved" or "I am being saved"?

And the story goes on that for the rest of the journey this great man of God explained to the simple believer the wonder and immensity of God's salvation—past, future and present.

"Jesus Christ, the same yesterday, and to day, and for ever" (Hebrews 13:8).

CHAPTER 4

JESUS CHRIST, GOD'S REMEDY FOR SIN

"Without shedding of blood is no remission" (Hebrews 9:22).

First of all, every one of us must recognize the fact of sin. People may use different names such as failings, weaknesses, hereditary tendencies, inhibitions, phobias, so on, but "Whatsoever is not of faith is sin" (Romans 14:23).

Often what we call a slight weakness in our own life we condemn as something more serious in someone else, but the Bible gets right down to the root of the matter and calls it "sin."

Some years ago in England the leading personality in a radio program called "The Brains Trust" was a brilliant atheist called Dr. Joad who had written many books denying the Christian faith. It was his delight to "take to pieces" any suggestion of belief, and time and time again he scored heavily at the expense of some simple believer. Then Dr. Joad fell ill and it took him many months to die. He died inch by inch, and while doing so he made a full survey of the Christian belief. His last book, *The Testament of Joad,* contains the admission that he could explain away everything in the Bible except SIN. In the end he believed what he had so often mocked–the fact of sin and the need of a Saviour from sin.

For any who talk of the discoveries of modern psychologists, it is important to realize that the Lord Jesus was the greatest psychologist who ever lived–He *knew* what was in man.

To many, the idea of the awfulness of God's judgment on sin is rather difficult to accept. Having been brought up on the idea "God is Love," it somehow does not seem to fit in. They fail to appreciate both the utter holiness of God, and secondly that God is other things beside Love.

For example in John's first epistle which tells so much of the love of God, before that subject is introduced we are faced in I John 1:5 with these words, "This then is the message which we have heard of him, and declare unto you, that God is light, and in him is no darkness at all."

Before we meet the God who is love, we have to deal with the God who is light. In John 1:4, 5 the Lord Jesus is shown as the Light that shineth in darkness. John 3:19 says: "And this is the condemnation, that light is come into the world, and men loved darkness rather than light, because their deeds were evil."

Bygone days of great revival have always been associated with the fearless presentation of sin, its vileness and its sure and certain penalty.

God's punishment of sin has been one of the consistent characteristics of His dealings with men, whether with individuals like David, Saul, Moses, and any other great Bible character—or with nations—Israel herself, as well as the annihilation of the foul-living nations in Canaan.

The greatest proof of God's judgment on sin is not the actual cross of Calvary, but the agony in the Garden of Gethsemane, when our blessed Lord faced the fact of "being made sin for us." How He shrank from the foulness of it, sweating as it were great drops of blood and praying "O my Father, if it be possible, let this cup pass from me" (Matthew 26:39).

As the great hymn writer Faber wrote:

> Ever when tempted, make me see,
> Beneath the olive's moon-pierced shade,
> My God, alone, outstretched, and bruised,
> And bleeding, on the earth He made.

24

And make me feel it was my sin,
As though no other sins there were,
That was to Him who bears the world
A load that He could scarcely bear!

It is essential to realize the unchangeableness of our God. Sin has not changed, neither has the attitude of God. What has changed is the national conscience. Things our forefathers believed in as pure and sacred are now laughed at, mocked and scorned in our modern Sodoms and Gomorrahs.

This challenges us to a personal identification with Christ. Many people will believe He died for us, but here the point is personal–confession of my sin–realization of my awful condition–identification with Christ as my Lamb.

"For he hath made him to be sin for us, who knew no sin; that we might be made the righteousness of God in him" (II Corinthians 5:21).

We are cleansed by his blood–I John 1:7.

We have redemption through his blood–Ephesians 1:7

We are made nigh by the blood of Jesus–Ephesians 2:13

We have been made to be at peace through the blood of his Cross–Colossians 1:20.

We have boldness to enter into the holiest by the blood of Jesus–Hebrews 10:19.

The phrase "The blood of Christ" and the teaching which involves reference to the shedding of His blood is frowned upon in many churches. It is considered unpleasant, decidedly "Old Testament," and definitely out-of-date.

One of the greatest successes the devil has had is to turn the hearts of many so called Christians against this teaching. They call it "the slaughter house religion."

But God does not ask our opinion on His plan for the remission of sins; He states the fact, and we can either take it or leave it!

As a schoolmaster for 30 years I have taught all age groups, and many subjects; but there are some things I never had to teach. I never had to teach a child to lie, or to swear, or to tell a dirty story. No one has ever had to teach a boy or girl to go into sin.

No one has to teach a teenager to break the moral codes and throw away honor and purity. No one has to teach a man or a woman to leave his home and family and enter into illicit relationships with others. No one ever has to teach these things–they are "built in" with the model. Jesus said: "For out of the heart proceed evil thoughts, murders, adulteries, fornications, thefts, false witness, blasphemies: these are the things which defile a man" (Matthew 15:19, 20).

It is interesting to notice that the word "proceed" is in the continuous tense–"they keep on proceeding." These are the words of the greatest psychologist who ever lived for He *knew* what was in man–He did not have to guess!

If we are honest, we have to acknowledge that this is true of our own hearts. There is a power of sin within us that overcomes us time and time again.

When was the first time you ever told a lie? How many lies do I have to tell to be a liar? One lie can keep you out of heaven! "And there shall in no wise enter into it any thing that defileth, neither whatsoever worketh abomination, or maketh a lie: but they which are written in the Lamb's book of life" (Revelation 21:27).

Most people will acknowledge the power of sin in their hearts, though they may call it some other name, e.g., personal failing, family weakness, natural tendency, etc. What most people overlook is the fact that, as well as the power of sin, there is also a penalty of sin. Every sin is a sin against Almighty God and "the wages of sin is death" (Romans 6:23). "The soul that sinneth, it shall die" (Ezekiel 18:4). "Your iniquities have separated between you and your God" (Isaiah 59:2).

Physical death is a physical separation from the physical world, but the death referred to above is spiritual death, both in this world and the world to come.

Notice: "The wages of sin *is* death–" *is* now, not will be in the future only. Because I am a sinner now I am

26

due, now, to go to a place of eternal separation from God. I don't have to lift a finger to go to a lost eternity—I am on my way already, and unless something happens to alter it, my end is both inevitable and incurable.

I John 1:9 says "If we confess our sins, he is faithful and just to forgive us our sins, and to cleanse us from all unrighteousness." God has a way of being both faithful and just—"faithful" to His essential character of LOVE and "just" to His essential character of HOLINESS—one of the great miracles of God.

God has devised the way. It is this—"Without shedding of blood is no remission" (Hebrews 9:22). These words form one of the essential key phrases of the word of God. Right from the beginning of Genesis to the end of Revelation the shedding of blood according to God's instructions is the only remedy for the penalty of sin.

Many people will say, "Yes, true, but that was the way of the Old Testament. Things have changed now." Yet the verb used is the present tense *"is* no remission" and it is written in the New Testament. God's demands have never changed and even today in the Atomic Age, without shedding of blood is no remission.

Chapter 4 of Leviticus, the Visual Aids section of the Word of God, details how a man could obtain forgiveness in the Old Testament. According to his social standing he had to bring an animal offering to the Lord. Before the beast was slain, the man placed his hands upon the head of the animal to identify the animal with himself.

The animal was then put to death instead of the man, and the shed blood was the proof of the pardon. The Bible says in Leviticus 4:35: "the priest shall make an atonement for his sin that he hath committed, and it shall be forgiven him."

The word *atonement* is very important; it implies literally "a covering." The shed blood covered the sin of the man so the man's sin could be forgiven.

While this method was wonderful it was also limited. If the offerer became conscious, at a later date, of the

27

burden of more sins he had to repeat the whole process again—a costly and humbling process. This fact is emphasized in Hebrews 10:4: "For it is not possible that the blood of bulls and of goats should take away sins." The man's sin remained, but it was covered.

Thus, under the Old Testament economy, all the sins remained for which offerings were made, they remained but they were covered by the shed blood. This fact throws into glorious relief the words of John Baptist: "Behold the Lamb of God, which taketh away the sin of the world!" (John 1:29).

What a stupendous thought. How precious is His precious blood. It could take away the sin of the whole world. All the sacrifices offered in the days of the Old Testament looked forward to Calvary's cross. Each animal was a type of God's lamb, but its shed blood could never take away sin; it simply covered it until the glorious day when God's own Lamb came, and by His shed blood took away the sin of the world.

Hebrews 10:1-18 brings out the truth concerning Christ: "Sacrifice and offering Thou wouldest not, but a body hast Thou prepared me" (verse 5). The body of Christ was specially prepared of God to be the offering for sin.

"We are sanctified through the offering of the body of Jesus Christ once for all" (verse 10).

"And every priest standeth daily ministering and offering oftentimes the same sacrifices, which can never take away sins" (verse 11).

"But this man, after he had offered one sacrifice for sins for ever, sat down on the right hand of God" (verse 12).

"For by one offering he hath perfected for ever them that are sanctified" (verse 14).

"And their sins and iniquities will I remember no more" (verse 17).

Notice the tremendous importance of verse 12—"One sacrifice for sins for ever." Calvary's cross is God's answer to all the sin of all time. Just as we look back to the cross

28

of Christ, so the Old Testament sacrifices looked forward to the cross of Christ.

They were the type but He is the Truth. The sins that were covered in the Old Testament were taken away by the shed blood of Christ. Notice how this magnifies the death of Christ so that we see it, not as one of God's afterthoughts, but truly as I Peter 1:19, 20 says—we are redeemed "with the precious blood of Christ . . . who verily was foreordained before the foundation of the world." Before ever the world was made, the precious shed blood of Christ was part of the divine counsel and strategy.

Revelation 5:9 says, "They sung a new song, saying Thou art worthy . . . for Thou wast slain, and hast redeemed us to God by Thy blood."

The center of the praise of Heaven is: "a Lamb as it had been slain" (Revelation 5:6) and the praise is: "Worthy is the Lamb that was slain to receive power, and riches, and wisdom, and strength, and honor, and glory, and blessing" (Revelation 5:12).

This praise becomes universal when we read in Revelation 5:13 "And every creature which is in heaven, and on earth, and under the earth, and such as are in the sea, and all that are in them, heard I saying, Blessing, and honor, and glory, and power, be unto him that sitteth upon the throne, and unto the Lamb for ever and ever."

That is what God and heaven think about the blood of Christ; no wonder the devil would seek to detract from such glory—even to the extent of getting so-called Christian ministers to scoff and belittle it.

The great question each person has to decide is— "What think ye of Christ?" (Matthew 22:42). Is He only a good man, a great prophet, a glorious example—or is He to be your Lamb? Remember our verse—"Without shedding of blood is no remission."

First there must be a conscious sense of my sin, and that I have sinned against Almighty God. My sin is an affront to the holiness of God and the penalty of sin is eternal separation from God.

Unless my sin is forgiven and taken away, it remains, so that I continue to live in my sins. If nothing is done to remove it I will die in my sins and be buried in my sins. Some day I will be raised, still in my sins, and before the Judgment Throne I will receive sentence of eternal damnation. All because, although I knew the remedy, I refused to apply it to myself.

It is just as if you were seriously ill, even to the point of dying, when a doctor came and placed some tablets in your hands. "Take these, and you will make a sure recovery. No one has failed to recover who made full use of this remedy," he says.

After he has gone, you put the tablets on your bedside table, you determine not to take them, and then eventually you die: Whose fault would it be? Surely your own. And if you go to a lost eternity having refused to take God's remedy it will be no one's fault but your own. "As I live, saith the Lord God, I have no pleasure in the death of the wicked" (Ezekiel 33:11).

When I come to the stage where I am conscious of the burden of sin, the horror of it, then I desire above all else to have remission of my sin. I must now do what is detailed in Leviticus Chapter 4. I must bring my Lamb and place my hands on its head; in other words, I must identify myself with Christ. I must claim Him personally as my Lamb of God. As Paul said of Him: "The Son of God who loved me, and gave himself for me" (Galatians 2:20).

I must realize that if I were the only sinner in the world then the shed blood of Christ would be needed to take away my sin. Having humbly and reverently identified myself with the Lamb of God I can now go on thanking and praising God for all He has done for me, just as the Ethiopian did when: "he went on his way rejoicing."

Notice that all this is an act of faith in God. We believe what God says: "without shedding of blood is no remission." We accept what God provides: "the Lamb of God." We do as God commands: identify with the Lamb and then, in faith, believe that God will keep His promise. "If we confess our sins, he is faithful and just to forgive us our sins, and to cleanse us from all unrighteousness" (I John 1:9).

The beauty of God's offer is that whosoever will may come. It is simple enough for everyone to understand. A clever university student once said to a preacher, "If I could only understand how God forgives sin I would accept it right away."

"But," replied the preacher, "if you could understand it because of your intellect, how would the young and the ignorant and the retarded ever come to a knowledge of forgiven sins? I have a missionary friend who has preached for over thirty years to the pygmies of the Congo forests, people apparently just one stage higher than animals. Even the men of the other tribes call them animals. How could they know forgiveness of sins?"

"Forgive me," the student said, "I never thought of it that way."

"No, *you* didn't," the preacher continued, "but God did."

"Whosoever will may come." Any one who feels a sense of sin is able to experience the blessing of forgiveness if only he believes what God says, accepts His offer, and claims Jesus Christ as his own personal Saviour, identifying himself with Him.

One thing more–God promises in II Corinthians 5:21 "For he hath made him to be sin for us, who knew no sin; that we might be made the righteousness of God in him."

God takes my sin and identifies it with Jesus, He who knew no sin, so that I might not only be forgiven, which is a neutral state, but that I might be made the righteousness of God in Him, a very positive position.

What an exchange–my sins for His righteousness! This is the white robe that the Apostle John saw worn by the great multitude in Revelation 7:9. The answer of the elder to John in Revelation 7:14 is so pointed: "These are they which came out of great tribulation, and have washed their robes, and made them white in the blood of the Lamb."

31

When we think of our own sin, the power of sin in our lives, then let us face up to the penalty of that sin. Let us hear God's remedy: *"without the shedding of blood is no remission."* Let us see God's Lamb–*that taketh away the sin of the world*. Let us reverently place our hands on Him, identifying Him with our sin, and us with His righteousness. We either look back to Calvary's perfection, or look forward to certain judgment.

This whole study of redemption by the blood is one which shows so clearly the oneness of the Word of God. What is taught in the New Testament is illustrated in the Old Testament: The type is in the Old Testament, the truth is in the New Testament.

The precious blood of Christ was foreordained before the foundation of the world (I Peter 1:20). Without the New Testament the sacrifices of the Old Testament would have no point and no direction. Without the Old Testament the sacrifice of Christ is meaningless.

As the New Testament so often says: "all this was done that the scripture might be fulfilled." The blood of Christ is the great link between the Old and the New. Let us get a holy sense of the greatness of the blood of Christ, don't apologize for it, don't seek to defend it. The shed blood of Christ is the unending wonder of the universe of God!

CHAPTER 5

THE POWER OF SIN

"For the law of the Spirit of life in Christ Jesus hath made me free from the law of sin and death" (Romans 8:2).

The last chapter dealing with the way God forgives the "penalty" of sin leads our thoughts quite naturally to the "power" of sin.

Usually when a person becomes a Christian, he experiences a moment of real decision, a time when he takes the vital step and becomes a living babe in Christ. Very often these decisions are moments of great emotional upheaval as the burden of sin falls off and the light of life falls upon once blind eyes. Surrounding the whole experience is a foretaste of glory–the peace of God blends with the joy of the Lord. At such a time the saved sinner will cry for joy and will witness to the fact that he knows he is saved because he can "feel" it.

Although this is a blessed moment it is also a dangerous moment. The saved sinner thinks–"This is it–how wonderful! I'll have this feeling for ever!"

But, as the days or weeks go by, the flash of emotional experience cools off, and the mountain top experience chills as we come down to the valley beneath. To one who is counting on feelings there comes tiny waves of doubt as the glow of an emotional conversion settles down to the ordinary every day life.

Then there comes a day when the sins, once knocked out, rise to fight again, and the babes in Christ discover to their horror that the power of sin is back again–sometimes stronger than before.

Very often there is a chill of shame as they realize that not only are the old sins back again, but that there is something in their own being which wants the sin and reaches out for it. This is a crucial moment of testing, because from this point in the soul's experience, back-sliding and coldness of heart can begin their withering plague.

Even though Christ met the penalty of sin, the power of sin is the daily problem in every Christian life. The greatest saints who ever lived had to face this problem—the power of sin in the life of the redeemed sinner. There will never come a day in your experience when sin will lose its power. Man by his behavior today is more wicked and cruel and sinful than ever before—certainly mankind hasn't improved.

Before the Second World War the modernists and the humanists used to preach that the way to produce a better man was by improving the environment. "Take people away from squalor and overcrowding and you will soon have a group of people developing the graces of the Christian life!" Such was their teaching then—now even the humanistic view of the inherent goodness of man is rather shaken.

Some men and women seek to escape from sin's power by entering the walls of a religious order. There, by leaving the world behind, they hope to be at perfect peace with God. But they, too, find that the wickedness of the world is not around them, but within them. Human efforts to handle this power of sin are varied.

Education was once considered to be the sure way to produce better people. "As people gain more knowledge and acquire more educated techniques they will see how bad it is to give way to sin." Such thinking is now out of date for all it produced was a race of clever devils.

Punishing the body to keep sin under control is still used by some people. Martin Luther, you will remember, flogged himself into insensibility in an attempt to deal with the power of sin. Self-punishment, to a greater or lesser degree, physically or mentally, is still used, but the effect is only for the moment as the center of interest is diverted from the sin to the self-suffering.

"Christianizing" a life is another way to meet the power of sin. By turning over new leaves, by making new resolutions, by following another rule or pattern, the struggler hopes for success.

The majority of people, however, seem to ignore the power of sin in themselves whatever they may say about others. To "put up" with the power and make the best of life is their answer. "After all," they say, "we are all in the same boat."

Romans 7:23 says:

> I see another law in my members, warring against the law of my mind, and bringing me into captivity to the law of sin which is in my members.

All of us know of the force of gravity, that unseen power which pulls everything down to the earth—nothing escapes its downward pull. So it is in our daily living. There is an unseen power which constantly pulls us down—a spiritual force of gravity. No one escapes its downward pull. Always and everywhere men and women and young people are under its power. The results of all our attempts to deal with the problem are the same.

There is that in us which is against God, which is not subject to His laws and which can never be made subject to His laws. It is profitless to try to live the Christian life under our own strength.

First, our fallen human nature can never rise up and be made subject to His laws. Secondly, not only can it not rise up, but it is always being pulled down by the spiritual force of gravity. It is interesting to see, at this point, how we differ from the Apostle Paul. He could say in Romans 7:18: "For I know that in me (that is, in my flesh) dwelleth no good thing." He recognized his utter worthlessness and he wrote himself off.

We, on the other hand, led by the philosophies of our day, believe there is *some* good in us. If we could only find our good points and develop them, then things would be different. Paul says, "In me–no good thing." We say, "Well, I know I'm not perfect but, after all I'm not as bad as all that!"

Paul was probably the greatest Christian who ever lived–and his humility proved it! As long as we are hoping to meet the power of sin by our own efforts, and to live a victorious Christian life through our own inherent good qualities, we are doomed to failure.

The answer to the problem of meeting the power of sin and living a victorious Christian life is not education or psychology, psychiatry or ethics, not even religion–it is a PERSON–JESUS CHRIST.

Have you ever realized that there has only been *one* really victorious Christian life in all the world's history–and that was the life of Christ Himself?

> John 8:46–"Which of you convinceth me of sin?"
> Hebrews 4:15–"In all points tempted like as we are, yet without sin."
> Hebrews 9:14–"Offered himself without spot to God."
> I Peter 2:22–"Who did no sin, neither was guile found in his mouth."
> I Peter 1:19–"A lamb without blemish and without spot."

His life was one constant victory over sin in all its power. Who else could say as He did in John 8:29 when speaking of His Father–"I do always those things that please him." Just think of it–always and in all ways those things that pleased God! One blessed victorious Christian life.

The only way for us to meet the power of sin is to realize more fully what we are told in II Peter 1:4: "Whereby are given unto us exceeding great and precious promises: that by these ye might be partakers of the divine nature. . . ."

When I become a Christian not only are my sins forgiven, but I become a partaker of the divine nature. Jesus Christ comes to live in me in the power of His Holy

Spirit. Many of us believe that we receive the Holy Spirit when we believe, but we only give this truth intellectual assent. We don't know why He comes and we are so busy living the Christian life and fighting sin that we have no time to find out.

Romans 8:9 says: "Now if any man have not the Spirit of Christ, he is none of his." So the Holy Spirit is the Holy Spirit of Christ. Christ Himself is the power of the Holy Spirit.

The Bible says I become a partaker of the divine nature. I already have one nature, a fallen human nature, which is "at enmity against God: for it is not subject to the law of God, neither indeed can be" (Romans 8:7).

So I now have two natures, a fallen human nature and the nature of the indwelling Spirit of Christ–the One who alone lived a victorious Christian life. One nature, which is sinful, is always being dragged down; the other, which is divine, is the resurrection life of Christ. One which can only fail, the other which can only succeed. But we have lived with the old nature so long that it is just "natural" to live that way.

Romans 8:2 has a wonderful promise: "For the law of the Spirit of life in Christ Jesus hath made me free from the law of sin and death." There is a new law which can make me free from the downward pull of the spiritual law of gravity, the law of sin and death. This law is the law of the Spirit of life in Christ Jesus, the upward triumphant victorious life of Jesus Christ.

What are the results of these opposite laws, operating as it were, at once? An example will help us understand.

Once I flew from Kennedy International Airport to London. As I walked from the airport buildings to the Boeing 707 Jet I was subject to the law of gravity. When I came to the steps leading up to the plane entrance door I had to climb up the steps using my power to raise my body up each step. On entering the plane I sat in the comfortable seat and just relaxed.

When all was ready the jet taxied to the runway, and after a while began to move down the long stretch ahead.

The speed increased second by second until, when it was moving about 150 miles per hour, it left the earth, and rose up into the night sky above New York.

The force of gravity against which I had climbed into the plane was still seeking to pull the plane down to earth–the whole 150 tons of it. But–there was another law in operation now against the law of gravity, a new law, the law of aerodynamics.

I knew nothing of the law of aerodynamics. I did not need to, but, because I was committed to the plane, and, because I was relaxing, I rose in triumph with the plane. The triumph of the jet was my triumph, its fantastic speed was my speed, all its possibilities were mine–because I was inside.

Thus it is with the law of the Spirit of life in Christ Jesus. I do not need to understand the theology to benefit–all I need to do is to commit myself spiritually to Jesus Christ as I did physically to the Boeing jet. Notice that it wasn't the quality of my faith that took me to London in six hours. A frightened passenger might spend the time in anxious fear, but he would get there just the same.

I am as strong as that in which I put my faith. If my faith is resting in Christ than I am as strong as He is.

Notice, too, I did not have to help the plane fly the Atlantic. It did not require any urging or pushing from me–the power was in the plane.

Similarly Jesus Christ can triumph in my life without help from me. It is when I interfere to "help" Him that things go wrong. Just imagine me, in my ignorance, at the controls of the Boeing jet! No, I just relaxed into the effortless perfection of the plane.

How then do we defeat the power of sin–with its downward pull–and rise to live a victorious Christian life? Surely the answer is simple. If I am in Christ and He is in me, as the Lord said in John 15:5, then my one job is to recognize this fact moment by moment and relate every circumstance to Him.

When the old temptations come with their seductive

38

attractiveness, I must not go out to meet them in my puny strength; I must commit it to Him in a quiet simple prayer. "Dear Lord, this temptation is too great for me to handle. I can only fail, Dear Lord; meet this for me in Your strength." Then leave it to Him. He will gain the victory through your yielded life.

Our faith will need to be so very childlike. We must abide in Him, rest in Him, and His will be the victory. Remember I John 4:4: "Greater is he that is in you than he that is in the world." The greatness isn't you or you plus Christ–the greatness is Christ alone. As we start to live this life of simple faith in the indwelling Christ things may seem a little awkward at first. Our natural impulse will be to get to work ourselves. We will need to cultivate His presence moment by moment to develop new behavior patterns.

Learn to thank Him for the blessing even before it comes. As the days go by, the practice of relating all to Him will become easier until, by His grace, we learn to trust Him in all things.

This does not mean that I just sit and do nothing, but that I expect Him to rule and over-rule in all my ways and all will be for His glory.

This does not imply any form of instant sanctification. As I practice these new behavior patterns, so I grow in grace. This is something I must practice and work at day by day. At first, there may seem to be no change in my life, but gradually, as I allow the Lord Jesus to live His life in me so the blessing is inevitable. There is no such thing as "instant springtime" but, if there is life, spring is inevitable.

Not that we can never go wrong. Remember the law of gravity is always in operation. If the law of aerodynamics ceases to function through loss of power, the force of gravity takes over and pulls a plane down to destruction. If I feel myself so much better that I step out in my own strength, down I will topple. If I do fail through self-effort. I must always make a point of telling Him immediately what a mess I have made. Then confess my sin, thanking

Him for His grace, go on to live for Him and through Him once more.

Thus, and only thus, can I come into the truth of what was studied in the second chapter, concerning the present tense of my salvation–"Daily delivered from sin's dominion by His resurrection life"–stand back and let the Lord Jesus live His life in and through me. It is His life, His victory, His peace, His power, His plan.

Christ never uses what is naturally good in us, otherwise we would have the glory. It must be Christ only. Paul could say in Galatians 2:20:

> I am crucified with Christ: nevertheless I live; yet not I, but Christ liveth in me: and the life which I now live in the flesh I live by the faith of the Son of God, who loved me, and gave himself for me.

Christ had taken over in Paul's life.

There has only been one really victorious Christian life, and this thought is very comforting to the weak. We do not have to follow a pattern lived by someone else, or compete against the "super-saints."

The only answer to the power of sin is the resurrection life of the Lord Jesus Christ.

"Christ is the answer to my every need."

CHAPTER 6

THE FALL OF MAN

"And the very God of peace sanctify you wholly; and I pray God your whole spirit and soul and body be preserved blameless unto the coming of our Lord Jesus Christ" (I Thessalonians 5:23).

We need to have a clear scriptural picture of man in his innocency so that, in the next chapters, the work of the Lord Jesus in the hearts of redeemed souls can be more fully appreciated. God said in Genesis 1:31: "And behold it was very good."

How wonderful, in every respect, must the first creation have been. With regard to the stories in Genesis, stories so often ridiculed, understand very clearly the point that when writing the Book of Genesis, the Holy Spirit wasn't writing a scientific treatise on anthropology. Basically the scientific references that can be deducted are correct, e.g. the order of creation. This order, which is so different from the fanciful fables of early human civilizations is correct by all modern standards.

The main purpose of the Book of Genesis is to show man in relationship to God, to show it in such a way that men of every social and educational standard throughout all the years of human civilization could see and understand.

The book is a triumph of divine ingenuity and skill. For thousands of years men and women have read it and understood its message, and have come into a right relationship with God. It speaks to the human heart in all its need.

Don't apologize for the Book of Genesis, don't defend the Bible. As one preacher said: "You don't defend a cage full of lions, just let them loose!" In simple faith believe God's Word, and you will find that there are many hungry hearts waiting to receive. To those who scoff and pour scorn—leave it with God—the Bible is the "sword of the Spirit." The Holy Spirit will use the Word of God as He wills.

If the ordinary man in the street is asked of what man is composed—apart from the wisecracks about bones, flesh, hair, etc.—the usual answer will be something like this; "I believe man is composed of body, soul and spirit." That seems to be the usual way of describing man—body, soul and spirit. This would be quite correct from the world's point of view because it gives the accepted order of importance in the world generally.

The body is, undoubtedly, the priority in the world's economy. All our activities are geared for a body-conscious generation—feeding it, clothing it, amusing it, transporting it, keeping it strong, and, finally, burying it.

The other two, soul and spirit, are relatively unimportant in the eyes of mankind. "After all," they say, "you can't even see them."

In I Thessalonians 5:23 the world's order is reversed. Man's spirit is first, then the soul and body. This part, the spirit of man, is that part whereby man can be God-conscious. Proverbs 20:27 says: "The spirit of man is the candle of the Lord." This is a very apt description of the human spirit—the candle, or the lamp, of God, because we see immediately that the spirit of man has no power in itself.

A lamp has a capacity to receive power and to turn it into light. If the power is there, the lamp can shine; if the power is turned off, it cannot light up. It is essential to grasp this truth—a lamp has no power in itself. In reality, it is not the lamp that burns but whatever is used as fuel or power.

We read in Genesis 2:7 that God breathed into man the breath of life, and turned on his lamp. As long as the breath of life was there, man would, and could, live and shine for God. Man is the only one in God's creation into whom God breathed the breath of life, because he was the only one who had a spirit, and who could be spiritually alive.

The word 'soul' is one about which many wrong conceptions exist. One common mistake is to confess the spirit with the soul, to use the names interchangeably. Hebrews 4:12 corrects this misconception. "For the word of God is quick, and powerful, and sharper than any two-edged sword, piercing even to the dividing asunder of soul and spirit." The human spirit and the human soul can be divided. Therefore, they cannot be the same. It might help us if we realized that sometimes the Bible uses the *heart* to mean the same thing as the soul. When the *heart* is used it obviously doesn't mean the pump within us which sends the blood circulating within our bodies, for in Psalm 14:1 we read: "The fool hath said in his heart, there is no God." And in Mark 7:21 the Lord declares that "out of the heart of men proceed evil thoughts." In Luke 12:19 the rich fool says: "And I will say to my soul, Soul, thou hast much goods laid up for many years." The best way to understand the meaning of the soul, or the heart, is to look upon it as the "life mechanism," the human personality of the individual.

The soul consists of three parts–the mind, the emotions, the will.

The mind contains all the powers of reasoning, and thinking, and understanding, and remembering. The emotions, which play such an important part in our relations to our fellow men, are our visible reactions to facts, situations and circumstances. The will is the executive of the soul, the finger on the trigger of the soul's response. The soul is that part of us which is self-conscious.

It comes as a surprise to some people to learn that an animal has a soul. Man has spirit, soul and body. Animals have soul and body. The members of the vegetable kingdom have only a body. All three groups are alive, but in three different degrees.

43

Consider the case of your dog, or your neighbor's dog. That dog has a soul, just as much as you and I have. It has a mind, it has emotions and a will.

Just think how clever some animals are, think how they can be taught tricks and also how many of them possess distinctive powers of reasoning. Certainly a dog has a mind, and it is an emotional animal. His tail is the visible indication of the feelings within. If you meet a strange dog who comes to you stiff legged and with his tail held stiff, and pointing straight up, you know immediately that there may be trouble at any moment. He is showing suspicion, doubt, and possibly annoyance. If, suddenly, the other end starts growling, you are facing a dog who is angry. When he is friendly his tail wags. If you speak severely to him, his tail droops and when he is thoroughly scared he tucks his tail between his legs. The full range of the dog's emotions are visibly displayed.

A dog also has a will of his own. I sometimes see a small boy taking a big dog on a leash for a walk. The boy wants to go up the road and so he pulls the dog along by the leash, but the dog wants to go down the road and he pulls the boy. The whole thing ends with the dog taking the boy for a walk.

The trees and flowers in your garden are alive, but they only have a body. They have no mind with which to think or reason, no emotions to display and no will to exercise. Flowers never decide to move to another part of the garden, nor do trees fall in love—but they are alive.

The body is the house in which we live. Job 4:19 says that men "dwell in houses of clay." I Corinthians 15:38, 39 says, "But God giveth it a body as it hath pleased him, and to every seed his own body. All flesh is not the same flesh: but there is one kind of flesh of men, another flesh of beasts, another of fishes, and another of birds." The body is the least important part of man, but not unimportant. II Corinthians 4:7 says of the Gospel of the grace of God, "But we have this treasure in earthen vessels, that the excellency of the power may be of God, and not of us." We are only earthen vessels, but we are holding

God's rich treasure. II Corinthians 4:16 says: "For which cause we faint not; but though our outward man perish, yet the inward man is renewed day by day." This emphasizes the transient nature of the body, perishing day by day. We really start dying the moment we are born.

The body with its appetites and desires is not sinful in itself. God put them there, they are part of His original plan. The trouble begins when we use, or abuse the body. Romans 6:16 says: "Know ye not, that to whom ye yield yourselves servants to obey, his servants ye are to whom ye obey, whether of sin unto death, or of obedience unto righteousness?"

The same hands that can bring healing through a doctor's skill can bring suffering through selfishness and bitterness.

The human body as we know it today is a fallen creation. Genesis 1:27, 31 says: "So God created man in his own image, in the image of God created he him; male and female created he them. And God saw everything that he had made, and, behold it was very good." Man as God created him was perfect, unstained by sin, living in complete harmony with his Creator.

Genesis 1:26 says: "And God said, Let us make man in our image, after our likeness; and let them have dominion. . . ." From this we see that the Holy Trinity was engaged in the creation of man–*Let us*. Man was made as a trinity himself–*in our image*–and man was made to have dominion over the rest of creation.

The Holy Spirit dwelt in man's human spirit as sovereign over all. Being in man's spirit He was in control of man's soul or heart. Thus the mind, and the emotions, and the will, came under the sovereignty of God. The Holy Spirit could teach man's mind, occupy his affections and control his will, thus divine righteousness was expressed in man's body. The dominion that man then exercised was in full accordance with the will of God.

God is love, this truth we know full well. But there is only one thing that love really desires and that is a free response from the object of the affections.

45

It is true on our human level that human love can only be satisfied when the love is returned. We can compel obedience but we cannot compel love. All the hard, weary work put in by a tired mother is amply rewarded when the little child looks into the mother's eyes, holds up its arms and whispers "I love you." Love can only be satisfied by love in return.

Thus it was with God. If man had been created as an robot he would have functioned perfectly in every way, always, but no robot can love.

Today men have designed and built huge machines that can "think" and "deduce"; their response is perfect, but there is no bond of affection between the machine and the man—the machine is truly soulless.

For man to be able to love he had also to be able "not to love." He had to have the power of choice, to be free to choose to love God or, if he so chose, not to love God. And so it was that God established the first tree of choice in the Garden (Genesis 2:16, 17). The tree of the knowledge of good and evil was the tree of choice. Everything else was for man, nothing was withheld, but at the tree of choice man had to show his love to God.

If he really loved God and wanted to serve and obey Him then, of his own free will, man would leave the tree alone. He would visibly demonstrate his love to God by his reaction to the tree of choice.

But this tree of choice also carried a penalty, for God said: "for in the day that thou eatest thereof thou shalt surely die" (Genesis 2:17). So it was that the first man, placed in the most beautiful garden there ever was, was presented with this choice.

Chapter 3 of Genesis details the way in which the devil in his antagonism against God came in, and by his evil suggestions was able so to influence the choice of man that the "fall of man" took place.

It is vitally important for us to concentrate on the fact of the choice that man made, because this same crisis comes often into our own lives.

We, too, are faced with a choice to be made, and the same tempter is ever at hand to present his side of the picture.

God had said in Genesis 2:17: "for in the day thou eatest thereof thou shalt surely die." The devil stated in Genesis 3:4: "Ye shall not surely die."

This was indeed a tree of choice, for Adam had to choose between the words of God or the words of the devil. Without this power to choose he could not visibly demonstrate his love to God, and yet because of this choice he could run the risk of incurring God's promise—*thou* shalt surely die. The story of the fall is, of course, the story that man believed the lie of the devil. In Genesis 3:4, 5 the devil said, "Ye shall not surely die: for God doth know that in the day ye eat thereof, then your eyes shall be opened, and ye shall be as gods, knowing good and evil."

What a temptation that was—to be godlike without be God-conscious. The Communists tempt the same way! They say to the peoples of the nations, "Rebel, you have nothing to lose but your chains!"

The devil suggested that God was denying them what could and should be theirs. "Ye shall be as gods!" Such was the devil's offer. It is good to pause here and see how true that has become in our day and generation. The cleverness of modern men is beyond description. They are indeed as gods in some of their fields of scientific discovery. They are indeed godlike, but they are not God-conscious. "There is no fear of God before their eyes" (Romans 3:18) and because "the fear of the Lord is the beginning of wisdom" (Psalm 111:10), they have no real wisdom whatsoever, just a race of clever devils.

Adam believed the devil, he chose to be godlike, he openly threw off his allegiance to his Creator believing, in doing so, that he had established his own freedom. What was the result? Did he die? God had said he would, the devil had said he wouldn't.

Adam woke up next morning, he could stand and move and think and talk. It seemed as though the devil was right! But although he was physically alive and soulishly active, he *was* dead, for God had switched off his lamp.

Remember, originally, the Holy Spirit dwelt in man's human spirit, thus controlling his heart. But when Adam disobeyed God, God withdrew His Holy Spirit from his spirit. Man died spiritually. ". . .as by one man sin entered into the world, and death by sin; and so death passed upon all men, for that all have sinned" (Romans 5:12).

Man devoid of God's Holy Spirit was dead, spiritually dead. Adam was now physically alive, soulishly active, but spiritually dead.

We read in Genesis 5:3: "And Adam lived an hundred and thirty years, and begat a son in his own likeness, after his image." Genesis 1:26 says: "And God said, Let us make man in our image, after our likeness."

Adam was the first man made in the image and likeness of God, but because of the fall, all the descendants of fallen Adam are in his likeness–physically alive, soulishly active, but spiritually dead. This state is called in the Bible "the natural man." Another translation calls it "the animal man," the man who functions as an animal.

I Corinthians 2:14 says: "But the natural man receiveth not the things of the Spirit of God: for they are foolishness unto him: neither can he know them, because they are spiritually discerned."

How true that is, God's things are foolishness unto him or her. The very fact that the unconverted person says, "But it doesn't make sense to me, it's all nonsense!" is a living proof that they are spiritually dead.

See now how John 10:10 links up with this. The Lord Jesus speaking of His own mission said: "I am come that they might have life, and that they might have it more abundantly."

God's salvation is not the forgiveness of sins, but the restoration of *life* on the basis of the forgiveness of sins.

The human body is not sinful of itself. Some people confuse it with the theological word "the flesh." The body needs to be cared for sensibly, not despised and ill-treated.

48

After all, God created the human body, and although sin and disease have weakened, and damaged the body, in some cases, it is still the work of the hands of God.

Remember, too, that the Lord Jesus took a human body, and lived, and died in it, and that He has taken that human body to heaven. The important point is—for what purpose is this body to be used?

When the Holy Spirit in man's human spirit controlled the mind, emotions and will, original man was perfect. Only the Lord Jesus has maintained that perfection of relationship even when tempted in the barren desert.

"The first tree of choice" was in the Garden of Eden, but Calvary's cross is "the second tree of choice."

We confirm or deny our relationship to God by our attitude to the cross of Christ. Everything in our case depends upon the choice we make. Adam was converted from life to death by his choice. We, in our day, can be converted from death back to life by our choice.

The beginning of Genesis is where the enemy has fought his greatest battles. The story of Adam and Eve and the fruit is ridiculed and laughed at. The enemy says: "Everyone knows this isn't true, it's only a fable!"

The great thing to realize is not the detail but the doctrine. This so called fable is repeated time and time again in our lives. The great question taught is "Who are you going to believe, God or the devil?" The great doctrine tested is: "Whatever a man soweth, that shall he also reap" (Galatians 6:7).

Notice also the lie of Eve at the end of Genesis 3:3: "God hath said, Ye shall not eat of it, neither shall ye touch it, lest ye die." When compared with Genesis 2:17 we find that Eve added the words "neither shall ye touch it." Adding our own words to a given statement is a common human failing and if we put words into the mouth of God which He never uttered, we may do great harm to His cause.

The obvious truth of this story is seen in the spiritual condition of man in our Atomic Age. The almost godlike power in the hands of men today is fantastic. One after

49

another he is unlocking the secrets of the creation of God. His scientific wisdom is phenomenal. Yet, when it comes to the simplest things of God he is as ignorant as the wildest savage is of nuclear fission.

Only a new creature, taught by the Holy Spirit, can understand even in a faint measure the mystery and the greatness of God.

CHAPTER 7

THE NATURAL MAN

"For I know that in me (that is, in my flesh) dwelleth no good thing: for to will is present with me; but how to perform that which is good I find not" (Romans 7:18).

The teaching of this chapter cuts across many of the accepted beliefs of modernism and humanism, for it shows that there is nothing good in man; that there is no divine spark of natural goodness which only needs to be developed.

This does not mean that some people are not naturally kind and loving. Some men and women seem naturally lovable just as some seem naturally mean and wicked.

Natural niceness can be the product of a good digestive system, or the result of careful upbringing by the parents. Often it is simply the result of the physical, psychological and nervous make-up of the individual.

Just as in animals some dogs are born mean, others are just as lovable and affectionate. The Word of God is quite definite concerning mankind, "for there is no difference: for all have sinned, and come short of the glory of God" (Romans 3:22, 23). "As it is written, There is none righteous, no, not one . . . there is none that doeth good, no, not one" (Romans 3:10, 12).

In the last chapter we thought of the fall of man, now we see what happened in men as a result of that fall.

A well-known preacher, famous for his Bible knowledge and for his quick and unusual wit, was once drawn into a conversation concerning a new baby.

51

He was asked to express his views on the baby's likeness to various members of the family, but he shocked the mother by quoting: "He is like his father the devil!"

That seems rather rude and cruel, and yet consider what Christ said. In John 8:30 is recorded the incident where our Lord was speaking to some Jews, good religious men who were attentive to His message. "As he spake these words, many believed on him." These people had responded in a way to His message. But it was to these same people—those who were good, respectable religious and believing, that in verse 44 Christ said, "Ye are of your father the devil, and the lusts of your father ye will do."

They had claimed in verse 41, "We have one Father, even God." Jesus replied in verse 47, "He that is of God heareth God's words: ye therefore hear them not, because ye are not of God."

It comes as a shock to realize that Christ taught not the Fatherhood of God, but the fatherhood of the devil!

These words were spoken to Jews—the chosen people of God, those who possessed all the laws and commandments of God, the descendants of faithful Abraham, possessors of all the promises of God, and they were spoken by the Son of God who did "always those things that please him" (John 8:29). They came as true words of condemnation, "ye are not of God." "Ye are of your father the devil." The proof of this, according to our Lord, was the family likeness, "the lusts of your father ye will do."

If this was true of believing Jews how true this must be of all men who are: "without Christ . . . having no hope . . . without God" (Ephesians 2:12). We are all of our father the devil, and the lusts of our father we will do. The family likeness is there, right from the beginning.

We know from Scripture that man was made in the likeness and image of the Trinity (Genesis 1:26). We have seen how Adam died spiritually in that God withdrew His Holy Spirit from man's human spirit.

The thing to remember now is that man in innocency was indwelt by God's Holy Spirit in man's human spirit. The Holy Spirit present in man was able to exercise sovereignty over the heart of man. He could teach man's mind, occupy his affections, and control his will.

Thus divine righteousness was expressed through man. Righteousness is God expressed in terms of man–God incarnate. The withdrawal of the Holy Spirit as the personal representative of God left a throne without a King, a kingdom without a Ruler, an area of unoccupied territory.

The devil had promised that man would be free, be as gods, that he could control his own life in every way. But, as we look around today we see that although man has cast off God, he is still in slavery, this time to sin.

As Paul says in Romans 7:19, "For the good that I would I do not: but the evil which I would not, that I do."

Man did become "free" of God in a sense, but only to enter into the "bondage of sin." The devil moved in to take possession, to stake a claim in man's soul. The devil thus expresses himself in man's activities. Sin in man is the devil in action. The words "the flesh" is that area of the devil's dominion, his kingdom in the hearts of men.

In Matthew 12:26 and 28 our Lord not only taught the fatherhood of the devil, but He also recognized the kingdom of the devil as well as the kingdom of God. A kingdom presupposes three things–first a king, then subjects, and thirdly the kingdom itself. Our study of the flesh in this chapter requires us to know a little about the kingdom of the devil. We speak generally of "The world, the flesh, and the devil," this is the Trinity of Hell, the substance of the kingdom of the devil.

In John 12:31 and John 14:30 our Lord twice called the devil "the prince of this world." In Luke 4:5-7 the devil offered our Lord the kingdom of the world and he said in verse 6, "All this power will I give thee, and the glory of them: for that is delivered unto me; and to whomsoever I will I give it."

He claimed that all the power and the glory was his, and Christ never corrected or challenged this statement. In Ephesians 2:2 he is called "the prince of the power of the air." I John 5:19 says, "the whole world lieth in wickedness" or as the Amplified Bible puts it, "the whole world [around us] is under the power of the evil one."

The devil's kingdom is the world system, all mankind without Christ, for he rules over the hearts of men, godless humanity.

Some of the references quoted on preceding pages emphasize the fact of this kingdom. The devil is called in Scripture *a murderer* (John 8:44), *a liar* (John 8:44), *a deceiver* (Revelation 12:9), *accuser* (Revelation 12:10), *tempter,* (I Thessalonians 3:5), *wicked one* (Matthew 13:19), *adversary* (I Peter 5:8)—all names which suggest corruption, evil and wickedness.

And if this is the character of the king we shall know what to expect from his kingdom. In John 7:7 our Lord said, "I testify of it, that the works thereof are evil." Christ had only condemnation and judgment for the world system, i.e. for Satan's Kingdom.

Christ's prayer in John 17 is full of such an attitude. He said, "I pray not for the world" (verse 9). "I have given them (his own) thy word; and the world hath hated them, because they are not of the world, even as I am not of the world" (verse 14).

Our Lord is not referring to the individual sinners who make up the world; to them His cry was "Come unto me" (Matthew 11:28). In John 15:19 Jesus said, "If ye were of the world, the world would love his own: but because ye are not of the world, but I have chosen you out of the world, therefore the world hateth you."

I John 2:15-17 says, "Love not the world, neither the things that are in the world. If any man love the world, the love of the Father is not in him. For all that is in the world, the lust of the flesh, and the lust of the eyes, and the pride of life, is not of the Father, but is of the world. And the world passeth away, and the lust thereof; but he that doeth the will of God abideth for ever."

The devil's subjects are unredeemed humanity—men and women without Christ—and the point of control is through the flesh. It is this foothold in human nature, this point of inside contact, this agency in the soul, that gives the devil his unbroken rule over the hearts of men and women.

Jesus said in John 8:44, "Ye are of your father the devil, and the lusts of your father ye will do."

In short, the devil is completely and utterly corrupt and wicked, so is his kingdom, and so are the subjects of his kingdom.

Now it is this flesh, this godless human nature, this which is utterly opposed to God, and with which God can have no dealings. It is this flesh which we seek to make attractive and presentable to God.

Galatians 5:19-21 lists for us the works of the flesh, "Now the works of the flesh are manifest, which are these: Adultery, fornication, uncleanness, lasciviousness, idolatry, witchcraft, hatred, variance, emulations, wrath, strife, seditions, heresies, envyings, murders, drunkenness, revellings, and such like."

Everything in this list bears the stamp of the devil, yet it is by the flesh we seek to serve God, by improving ourselves, by developing our latent qualities. All is the flesh and all is against God.

There are other names applied to this area of the devil's dominion. Sometimes it is called "the old man" or "the body of death"–the implication being that it is "the old nature" or the "spiritually dead part." It is also called "the carnal mind"–carnal here meaning "of the flesh."

The great thing to realize is that there is a state of perpetual enmity between God and the flesh. "So then they that are in the flesh cannot please God" (Romans 8:8). "Because the carnal mind is enmity against God: for it is not subject to the law of God, neither indeed can be" (Romans 8:7).

Notice the last four words in Romans 8:7–*neither indeed can be*. It is impossible to make the flesh acceptable to God.

"For the flesh lusteth against the Spirit, and the Spirit against the flesh: and these are contrary the one to the other" (Galatians 5:17).

Notice the word Spirit has a capital, the Holy Spirit. The devil has got his fifth column–the flesh–in every human heart.

It is good at this point to pause and remember what the Lord said in John 14:30, "for the prince of this world cometh, and hath nothing in me." The Lord's body was perfect humanity.

Like the original first Adam, there was no area of "the flesh," no area in his personality where the devil had a foothold. There was no "fifth column"in the life of our blessed Lord.

The "flesh" is all that a man is without Christ.

What religion seeks to do is to somehow make an offering to God. Being of the world it takes the things of the world. It takes "the flesh" and proceeds to dress it up, to deck it out and make it lovely to look at. It covers "the flesh" with beautiful thoughts, color, impressive music, and ritual. Everything looks good to the eye, sounds good to the ear, so it must be good–but it is flesh, all flesh.

God's Word says, "God is a Spirit: and they that worship him must worship him in spirit and truth" (John 4:24). Also, "the natural man receiveth not the things of the Spirit of God: for they are foolishness unto Him: neither can he know them, because they are spiritually discerned" (I Corinthians 2:14).

Notice the words–*neither can he know them.* There is no possibility that the natural man can ever know the things of God. What is the natural man referred to here? Really it is the flesh, it is man without the Spirit of God.

The French Bible translates "the natural man" as *L'homme animal*–the animal man–the man who is like an animal, in that there is only the body and the soul functioning.

As we saw in the previous lesson, the natural man or the unbeliever is fallen man. He is physically alive, soulishly active, but spiritually dead.

His flesh is the area of his soul which dominates his body. His soul is his mind, his emotions and his will, and man is on the throne–so he thinks.

He boasts of his freedom, of how he can please himself. He gives in to his lusts as and when he pleases, it is the "natural" thing to do because he is a "natural" man. Notice that his lusts may not be only vile and filthy. The word lust means overdesire. Some men and women lust for power in business or home. Some lust for beauty, art and education to the exclusion of other things–an overdesire.

But at the back of every man's desire is the devil. Man may be on the throne, but it is the devil who is the power behind the throne. The devil has taken all the normal desires and needs of the human heart, and overstressed, and overdeveloped them until the ordinary things of life bear his mark.

One of the greatest shocks that can come to a simple believer in Christ is to realize that "the flesh" still exists after conversion. During the first flush of joy of sins forgiven the new believer sometimes makes the error of imagining that his Christian life will be joy and peace all the way.

Then, after a period of days, weeks or months, the devil comes back again to tempt through the flesh, the same old way, and the believer suddenly realizes that something in him responds to the old lusts and worldly pleasures, and, more than that, it not only responds but it wants again the old things and the old ways.

Like the children of Israel, as detailed in Numbers 11:5, 6, "We remember the fish, which we did eat in Egypt freely; the cucumbers, and the melons, and the leeks, and the onions, and the garlic. But now our soul is dried away: there is nothing at all beside this manna, before our eyes." They looked back to the things that gave them pleasure. They forgot the lashes and the slavery. They despised the heavenly provision. I Corinthians 10:11 tells us these incidents concerning the children of Israel were written for us as types and warnings.

When the flesh moves within the believer producing these desires and lusts for past sins, the child of God is greatly tested. Sometimes he wonders whether he ever was converted, or whether the whole thing was a fake or a fraud.

But far from proving that his conversion was a fraud it emphasizes the fact that it was real. Galatians 5:17 says, "For the flesh lusteth against the Spirit, and the Spirit against the flesh: and these are contrary one to the other: so that ye cannot do the things that ye would."

The unbeliever is never conscious of such an inward battle. His lusts have long since stifled the voice of his conscience–God's built-in warning system–so that his life is a progression of adventure into lusts (i.e. overdesires) as opportunities occur, circumstances arise, and the devil drives.

The correct thing to do is to realize that what is born of the flesh is flesh and always will be flesh. You cannot alter it, improve it or develop it. It will always be opposed to God and God's things. The Word of God teaches us how to handle it. Galatians 5:24 says, "and they that are Christ's have crucified the flesh with the affections and lusts."

Paul says in Galatians 2:20, "I am crucified with Christ"–meaning the flesh, the area of the devil's control. We are instructed in Romans 6:11, "Likewise reckon ye also yourselves to be dead indeed unto sin, but alive unto God through Jesus Christ our Lord."

Our problem is that as fast as we reckon the "self-life," the "flesh" to be dead, the devil seeks to revive it.

There is no such thing as the eradication of the old nature, or sinless perfection; the Bible teaches that God never removes the old nature, but He does provide the remedy.

We can be "alive unto God" but only "through our Lord Jesus Christ." As we saw in the last chapter we are made partakers of the divine nature (II Peter 1:4)– Jesus Christ lives in us in the Person of His Holy Spirit.

Where Christ is in control there is peace, whether it be during the storm on the sea, or in the maniac from the tombs–He is the author of peace.

So in our lives if we recognize the sinfulness of the "flesh," and cease our efforts of self-improvements, recognizing the truth that we are *new creatures in Christ* (II Corinthians 5:17), we will remove much of the heartache and frustration from our Christian living.

Not I but Christ—In me no good thing—I can do all things through Christ. We must recognize ourselves for what we are, and thank Him for what He is.

"Sin shall not have dominion over you" (Romans 6:14) if you yield yourselves unto God.

We must remember continually that God has "written off" human nature. He has made no attempt to select good parts to repair the damage of sin. *If any man be in Christ he is a new creation.*

The presence of the indwelling Christ is the perfection and the purity and the peace. This teaching is utterly opposed to the indefinite philosophies of much modern teaching. To realize this is to understand yourself.

God is not shocked at *our* continual failure, it is no surprise to Him. So long as we try to improve our flesh then so long will we know continued heartache and frustration. The greatest saints of God have all had a tremendous sense of their own personal unworthiness—which in consequence, cast them more on the sufficiency of Christ.

We need to realize how malignant is the cancer of sin in the flesh, yet how perfect is the inworking of the indwelling Holy Spirit of Christ.

Christ never prayed for world peace, instead he called people out of the world system. This should set us thinking of how different was the mind of Christ from many of the world organizations for peace. He was not of the world, and yet He was in the world seeking the lost.

"The flesh" is anti-God—"it lusteth against the Spirit"—its works are of the devil—and yet the natural man ever seeks to make it presentable to God. He wants to worship God with the flesh in spite of the words of Christ in

59

John 4:24, "God is a Spirit: and they that worship him must worship him in spirit and in truth." How cleverly the devil uses his agency to keep man from God.

While it is no excuse for sin, it is a sure comfort to realize that although temptation comes through the flesh, temptation itself is no sin, nor is it a cause for doubting your salvation. Very often there is a fiercer strife within the human heart after the decision has been made for Christ than before. This fierce strife is a proof of the indwelling Spirit striving against the flesh, convicting of sin and seeking to purify the temple.

The only answer to this battle of the believer is to yield all to Christ, to let Him move into every area of the human personality, mind, emotions and will, so that there may be a personal experience of the truth of Romans 8:37, "Nay, in all these things we are more than conquerers through him that loved us."

CHAPTER 8

SEPARATED TO CHRIST

"Herein is my Father glorified, that ye bear much fruit; so shall ye be my disciples" (John 15:8).

One of the greatest supporters of separation is the devil himself. He has developed the technique of separation to a fine art. Wherever he comes across a group of Christians who are keen, alert and getting on with the job, the most effective way he has of making them nonproductive is to get them all tied up with separation.

The more he can get them "separating from" the more successful is his plan. It can sound so good, so "Christian" and so "holy" when really it is so completely negative.

Jesus said: "I, if I be lifted up . . . will draw all men unto me" (John 12:32). His approach was entirely positive.

Many people think in terms of "we don't do this, we don't go there, we can't wear that." This is the way the world judges, but it is utterly fruitless. The Lord said: ". . . by their fruits ye shall know them" (Matthew 7:20).

It is interesting to discover what the various nations and denominations think of "separation."

In America smoking and drinking are not generally practiced by convinced Christians, but cosmetics can be freely used. In Britain smoking and drinking are generally "out," and cosmetics are only just coming "in." In Germany smoking and drinking can still be used but cosmetics are definitely "out." Other diverse views are taken regarding movies, the wearing of hats by ladies, the wearing of shorts or slacks by ladies, the non-wearing of stockings by ladies, the color of men's Sunday clothes and shoes.

In each case, the emphasis is deflected from positive growth, it is separation from this, and this, and this. The process is entirely negative and to practice it effectively we must keep checking and looking *at* the things from which we are separated.

But being "separated to" is the positive position, where a Christian looks to the object of his separation. In John 8:12 Christ said: "I am the light of the world: he that followeth me shall not walk in darkness. . . ." If we imagine the physical act of following a light we can easily see that our pathway is illuminated as we go. If we turn aside or turn our backs on the light the very act of putting ourselves between the light and our pathway causes us to walk in a darkness, our own shadow!

In John 15:1-11 our Lord is teaching the secret of positive separation. He calls it "abiding." His perfect illustration is the branch abiding in the vine. The branch belongs to the vine, the vine belongs to the branch–they are "separated" to each other. Abiding is separation and separation is abiding. Notice that abiding is not "doing nothing"; it is a positive act whereby the branch becomes a channel through which can flow the life of the vine. Abiding is inevitably bound up with fruitfulness. Where there is no abiding there is no fruit. This, as our Lord taught in John 15:5, is the relationship between the believer and the Lord.

As one views the lives of many Christians it is obvious that with many of them there is a real desire to be fruitful. Many are ready and willing to give of their time, labor and money to help in the cause of fruitbearing–whether it be personal fruitbearing or the fruitbearing of a church or Sunday school.

In nearly every case the believer is earnestly trying to produce fruit to the glory of God. Many churches are united in their one desire to produce more fruit than last year.

How much heartache would be spared if we realized that our Lord taught that the branch did not *produce* the fruit–it *bore* the fruit. The fact that we are called not to produce fruit but to bear fruit is the great secret of abiding.

The branches do not have to turn and twist, to struggle and strive, in order to squeeze out the grapes, instead the branch abides, and the life of the vine flows into and through the withered looking vine branch, and in God's good time, in cooperation with all other aspects of God's creation the fruit is borne.

Jesus taught that there were three degrees of fruitfulness–fruit, more fruit (verse 2), much fruit (verses 5, 8). The basis of all is abiding, but the degree differs as our relationship deepens.

Verse 2 teaches us that "bearing fruit" is the natural result of abiding "in Him." Obviously the branch must be *in* the vine before the sap can flow. But the first verse teaches that the Father is the husbandman, the gardener, who seeks to bring his vines to peak production and then to keep them in that state.

At the same time, Christ says that any branch that is bearing no fruit at all is taken away. If there is not one single grape then the branch is removed–but this would be a rare event. Most branches can and do bear, at least, a few grapes. There can hardly be a single true Christian who is utterly fruitless. The grapes may be few and small, but there is fruit.

Notice now what the Father does to a branch bearing only "fruit"–He prunes it. Just as the gardener will cut back here and cut off there, so God operates in our lives. The result of the gardener's work is to "limit" the branch, to make it smaller, to remove the long showy growths. When he has finished the branch will be a sorry sight–clipped, sawn and cut–but by his skillful hands the branch is prepared for more fruit next season.

So God often operates in our lives. If we abide we may be pruned. We may feel that our lives are being cramped, we may be losing connections here, or our efforts in one direction may suddenly come to a stop. Suffering may enter our lives, sorrow and loss may come. God is not being cruel or spiteful or vicious—He is preparing for "more fruit." Remember that the One who prunes the tree, holds the shears and the knife. Hebrews 12:6: "For whom the Lord loveth He chasteneth, and scourgeth every son whom he receiveth."

While "more fruit" is certainly an improvement over "fruit," the target is "much fruit." Many of us learned in our catechism that "Man's chief aim is to glorify God, and to enjoy Him for ever." That is very true. Every Christian's chief aim should be "to glorify God." See how this links up with verse 8 in our passage: "Herein is my Father glorified, that ye bear much fruit." God is only glorified in our lives when we bear much fruit. It is interesting to remember that in Luke 2:8, the shepherds were abiding. In verse 14 the angels announced glory to God in the highest. In the manger was the divine "much fruit."

If pruning brings "more fruit," what then is the secret of "much fruit"? The secret is detailed for us in verse 5 of our passage: "He that abideth in me, and I in him, the same bringeth forth much fruit." When we compare this verse with verse 2, we see that in verse 2 there is fruit when "the branch is in me." But verse 5 has an addition to verse 2, not only is there "He that abideth in me," but there is "and I in him." This is the key. The Lord says when "I am in Him," as well as "he in me" then there is the "much fruit."

This, first of all, is a deepening of relationship. When I am "in Christ," I am safe. I have been born again and have come into a new relationship.

In one sense, it is a one way traffic, for all the blessings are mine. But when we recognize that not only am "I in Him" but in a more wonderful way "He is in me" then my relationship is deepened. My abiding is more complete and peaceful.

This world, then takes its proper place in my sense of values and in my order of priorities. I cease to plan to produce fruit and can now afford to abide to bear "fruit," then "more fruit," and then "much fruit." The Lord adds these words on the end of verse 5, "for without me ye can do nothing"–not even one thing.

This spotlights the real heavenly value of much of our "fruit production." It may seem in our eyes that our plans, our programs, our personalities have made a great hit. Numbers were enlarged, offerings were increased, our targets were passed. But is this not "fruit"–let alone "more fruit" or "much fruit."

Fruit is not produced *by* the branch, it is borne *on* the branch by the life of the vine working *in and through* the branch. So then "much fruit" is not produced by my efforts but I become the channel through whom flows the life of Christ. Fruit bearing ceases then to be my responsibility. I simply become the channel, the vehicle, through whom Christ can operate in His Risen Life.

Remember, true separation is not negative, but very positive. True separation is "abiding," the only source of fruitfulness.

This stand on separation will solve and answer many of the questions that are perplexing young Christians. If I am truly and sincerely separated unto Christ, wanting Him first in all things, for His pleasure and glory always– then many of the problems would never arise.

"These things have I spoken unto you, that my joy might remain in you, and that your joy might be full" (John 15:11).

The fullness of joy comes with the "much fruit" which in turn can be our experience as we realize the Person of the indwelling Christ. Not that I am indwelt by some kind of Holy Spirit of which I know nothing–but that Christ my blessed Saviour lives in me, so that all that "He is" can be expressed through my life in terms of my yielded humanity.

CHAPTER 9

THE CALL TO SERVICE

"That Christ may dwell in your hearts by faith"
(Ephesians 3:17).

This chapter will come as a challenge to many readers
as to whether they really mean business with God. So
many people play at "being Christians," dressing up for
the part, learning their words, correcting their exits and
entrances, so that as they strut on the world's stage they
play their part very well–they become good actors. But
when the costliness of the Christian life is considered
they shrink from the consequences.

Some one has said that, concerning the Christian life,
the entrance charge is nothing but the annual subscrip-
tion is everything.

Let this chapter then search your heart so that you
may experience a deeper relationship with your Lord. To
be a real Christian certainly can be costly, but the wonderful, glorious thrill of knowing Christ abiding in the heart
is treasure beyond compare.

Man in innocency lived his perfect dependent life
before God. We saw that, as in Genesis 2:7: "man became a living soul," so the Holy Spirit in man's human
spirit was able to move into the area of his soul, or heart,
controlling and guiding man's mind, emotions, and will.
There was thus a unity of peace and purpose, and the
Holy Spirit was manifest in man's human body.

But when man believed the lie of the devil he died,
spiritually, and the Holy Spirit was no longer controlling
and guiding in the trinity of the heart. Man had been

promised freedom by the devil but the human heart became a kingdom without a king; there was a throne unoccupied. It was then that man became "as gods." The big "I" took over the kingdom of the heart, and self sat upon the throne.

The plan of God's redemption, as it affected man, was two-fold. First to deal with the sinfulness of the situation, and secondly to restore life to the spirit of man in order to re-establish the communion first broken by Adam. That plan has been fulfilled at the cross of Calvary, as we read in I Peter 1:19, 20 that we were redeemed "with the precious blood of Christ, as of a lamb without blemish and without spot: who verily was fore-ordained before the foundation of the world, but was manifest in these last times for you."

Ephesians 3:14-21 contains the prayer of progress in practical Christianity. In verse 14 Paul says—"For this cause"—this is the reason for his prayer. Notice also how in verse 16 he asks a blessing—"according to the riches of his glory"—not out of His riches but according to. A father who was in deep poverty might struggle hard to get enough to buy his child a Christmas present. He might eventually buy something very cheap, but the child would be satisfied. If a millionaire was to give his child a similar present the child would despise it. He would want a gift according to his father's riches. Both would give their best according to their riches—but how different the best would be. So, with God, He gives according to His riches.

In verse 16, Paul asks that we might be strengthened with might by His Spirit in the inner man; that into the human spirit may come the strengthening, reinforcing, mighty power, of the Spirit. Remember that the Spirit is the Spirit of Christ. "Now if any man have not the Spirit of Christ, he is none of his" (Romans 8:9). Jesus said in John 10:10: "I am come that they might have life, and that they might have it more abundantly." This is *the* life, Christ Himself, The coming of the new life means the coming of a new birth so the man is born again.

67

When Christ is received by faith, then that soul is born of God. Whether they realize or understand this, or not, this is what happens when any soul receives Christ as Saviour–into the human spirit comes the mighty power of the Holy Spirit of Christ.

The receiving of life in the human spirit is only the beginning of the prayer. Paul then goes on in verse 17–"That Christ may dwell in your hearts by faith." If this also takes place then there would be a restoration of the blessed relationship as at first. The Holy Spirit would then be free to move into the human heart to guide and control in the affairs of mind, emotion, and will. Unfortunately what often happens is that the sinner in all his need eagerly accepts the forgiveness offered by God. He is happy to be born again. But then comes a full stop. The big "I" is still on the throne, choosing and deciding–possibly not now in lusts of the flesh but choosing the directing of the spiritual life. "I" gets busy planning and preparing, using all the resources of mind, emotions and will to put on a good show and live the Christian life.

It is at this very point that the first big challenge can come.

Verse 17 says: "That Christ may dwell in your hearts . . ."–dwell there, abide, settle down, live there.

Depending on our own personality we can have different ways of inviting people into our own homes. If someone knocks on the door and we go to find a complete stranger, we will probably leave him outside while we attend to his request.

Perhaps someone may come who lives in our street, way down at the other end, and when we open the door to greet them we react differently. The visitor is not a complete stranger, but a semi-acquaintance, and so we invite them in, but only 'just in.' We ask them to wait there–on that spot–while we attend to their request.

Possibly when the door is opened another time we find someone we know, from the office or store. Here there is a progression in acquaintanceship so there is a progression into the house. Possibly they will be invited into a room—but only one room.

But, of course, if the visitor is one of the family and he abides in the house he doesn't knock, he walks in, he goes where he wants because the house is his.

How far does Jesus Christ get into your house? Paul prayed: "That Christ may dwell, or abide, in your hearts." The chapter on fruitfulness taught us that: "He that abideth in me, and I in him, the same bringeth forth much fruit" (John 15:5). The vital point is whether Christ abides in me so that there can be "much fruit." Paul prayed that this blessed experience could be ours— but here is the challenge—the greatest challenge any soul can face. It will bring a new standard of values—His standards—for He said: "They are not of the world, even as I am not of the world" (John 17:14).

If Christ comes to abide in my heart something will have to happen. Jesus Christ will have to have complete control of my mind, thoughts, ambitions. He will want to control what comes into my mind—what books I read, what T.V. programs I see. He will want to control where I go, and with whom I am friends.

II Corinthians 10:5 faces us with a tremendous challenge—"bringing into captivity every thought to the obedience of Christ."

Christ in control means thoughts in captivity. Nothing impure or unholy can stay where He is. This is the price of purity of mind—that Jesus Christ shall cleanse and remove all that offends Him. Our prayer should be— "Come in to my mind, blessed Lord, show what is false and impure and cleanse it by Thy Holy Spirit. Set a watch at the door so that all that enters has first been brought to You, for Your divine approval."

If we really mean business, and truly want Christ to abide in our hearts, we must realize that there are many things that will need to go.

If Christ is to abide in my heart, not only will He control my mind but also my affections must be at His disposal. If I think of my emotions as a piano keyboard, we can well see the full range from a bass of bitter anger, right through to a tranquil treble.

But if Christ played the melodies on the strings of my emotions some of our regular "concert pieces" would never be heard again The peace of Christ abiding in my heart would demonstrate the love of Christ in my daily living. Possibly in no other sphere is Christ's presence more quickly shown than in the emotions. Hand over your quick temper and bitter tongue for Christ to deal with. Make apologies, obey parents, respect teachers! As Christ dwells in us, His Spirit gives us the power to carry out His commands.

The will is like the finger on the trigger of my response —a slight pressure and unending trouble can follow. Christ must abide in my will, also, and just as He could say to His Father: "Not my will but thine be done," so I must say the same to Him.

The will is the throne of the heart, but with many Christians "I" is still in control. If Christ is to abide, then He must be on the throne. "If Christ is not Lord of all, then He is not Lord at all."

Paul continues his prayer: "And to know the love of Christ, which passeth knowledge, that ye might be filled with all the fulness of God" (Ephesians 3:19).

This means our spirits, souls and bodies–all filled for Him.

And we should not fear what this could mean for verses 20 and 21 say:

Now unto him that is able to do exceeding abundantly above all that we ask or think, according to the power that worketh in us, unto him be glory in the church by Christ Jesus, throughout all ages, world without end. Amen.

All God desires from us is a willingness to be obedient. He will do above all we ask or think by the power of the indwelling Christ. As we open the door of our hearts, allowing Him to move from room to room cleansing, purifying, burning out, we shall experience the truth of the Lord's words in Matthew 5:8: "Blessed are the pure in heart: for they shall see God."

Our continual prayer should be: "Blessed Saviour, Thou hast died to redeem me to Thyself. Show me now my utter selfishness and unworthiness. By Thy Holy Spirit create in me a hunger for Thy abiding presence. Make me willing to open every door in my heart to Thy searching gaze, then show me Thy will for my life. Finally give me Thy willingness to do, Thy courage to dare, and Thy joy to set my heart rejoicing. Amen."

CHAPTER 10

THE COST OF SERVICE

"But made himself of no reputation, and took upon him the form of a servant, and was made in the likeness of men" (Philippians 2:7).

Many Christians today are busily engaged in serving the Lord under the wrong terms of service. In some cases they regard the service itself as the object of their Christian life; the act is made the end and not the means to an end. As long as they are engaged in a busy round of church activities they are satisfied with their service. As long as they can point to membership of this society and that society, on the committee of this group and that group, their consciences are at rest—they are busy serving the Lord.

This chapter is an attempt to analyze Christian service in it simplest terms and then to see how we fit into God's plan.

First, let us see what service is *not*.

America today, more than ever before, is a land of big business. Millions of dollars are invested in the training of staff, in research in the preparation of the product, analysis of market, advertising of goods, etc.

Yet big business is not a philanthropic society; all these dollars are invested and spent with the ultimate object of acquiring a return. As long as returns are greater than expenditure then the company can make a profit and survive, but if the returns drop for too long the company will have to fold up.

If we looked at Christian service as a big business what

tremendous activity we would find! There is expenditure of millions of dollars, training of staff, advertising of goods–but there the comparison ends. The visible results in many fields of Christian service are pitiful compared with the expenditure. From a business point of view, much Christian service in many churches is practically useless–unless the ultimate aim is to keep the members on the move.

But what fruit is there for Christ? Much of this misguided service comes from imitation of the world. Jesus said: "They are not of the world, even as I am not of the world" (John 17:14).

The Lord's methods were so different from the accepted standard of His day. He was revolutionary in His ways, His works and His teachings. Today we tend to copy the best ways of the world in our techniques, but He broke away from accepted techniques and tradition.

The whole secret of the Lord's life of service is hidden in Philippians 2:7.

See, first, these words: "But made himself." All things were made by Him and the last thing He made was "Himself of no reputation." He was rich, He was Deity, and yet He emptied Himself of power, and He stripped Himself of His glory. He took the first step–"He made himself."

Secondly, the verse goes on to say "He was made." We must be careful not to miss the absolute simplicity of this. Many of God's great lessons are very simple, in fact, so simple we overlook them. This verse is an excellent example.

The words, "He made himself," are in the active voice in the English grammar. This means that He was the one who did the actual making. He initiated the process.

Conversely, the words, "he was made," are in the passive voice in the English grammar. This means that other people did the making. His hands were off His own life. He was the one who was made.

In other words, having taken the first step of "making Himself" He was then subject all His life to "being made" by others (all, of course, under the divine will of Almighty God).

Notice how limited He was. He was born a helpless baby, dependent on his parents. He was made a refugee as an infant, was made to flee to Egypt. They made Him carry His cross at the end. And all through His blessed life He was subject. He had taken His hands off His own life, and He was going to take the consequences.

But how wonderful is Philippians 2:9. The ultimate end to His subjection was exaltation–above *every* name– with every knee bowed and every tongue confessing. Our hearts cry, "Hallelujah!"

Why was this passage in Philippians written? As an encouragement of a "happy ending"? Verse 5 contains a command: "Let this mind be in you." This is no trivial request but a divine command from Almighty God. The example has been shown, the pattern has been proved. God has been satisfied, and now the word comes to you and me: "Let this mind be in you." We, too, have to take these steps that the Lord took.

First, there must be a moment in our lives when we realize God's perfect plan of service, when we are willing to humble ourselves and to "make ourselves." We must deliberately take our hands off our own lives and, regardless of the consequences, accept the second step of the perfect plan of God, become willing to "be made."

This comes as a costly challenge to every man or woman because all the glamor and the glory is gone and we are left with the chill of obedience.

In the story of the Prodigal Son in Luke 15:11-24 we can see how the two stages in the boy's life are revealed in verse 12: "Give me," and verse 19: "Make me." At first it was all "give me"–all for self. Later on, as God worked in his heart, he speaks those precious words– "make me. . . ."

Many of us are like the son before he came to God in our service. We are "give me Christians," always doing and going and getting. But Philippians 2:7 is very clear;

there are just two simple steps: make ourselves nothing; then be made.

As Christians we so often seek to gain a reputation, as a good organizer, a good singer, a regular attender, a cheerful giver. The trouble with gaining a reputation is that we want to keep the reputation that we have gained. So, in the end, our Christian service is concerned with doing things so that I will live up to my reputation! Christ made Himself of no reputation—dare we!

Paul followed Christ. He said in I Corinthians 9:19, and 22:

> For though I be free from all men, yet have I made myself servant unto all, that I might gain the more . . . To the weak became I as weak, that I might gain the weak: I am made all things to all men, that I might by all means save some.

Here is the secret of Paul's service—"I made myself" (verse 19) and "I am made" (verse 22).

Just as the service of Christ ended in the exaltation so, too, will ours.

> His lord said unto him, Well done, thou good and faithful servant: thou hast been faithful over a few things, I will make thee ruler over many things: enter thou into the joy of thy Lord (Matthew 25:21).

To the one who, like the son in Luke 15, has said, "Make me . . ." will come the words of the Master, "Well done, thou good and faithful servant."

We must realize continually how completely different is God's plan from the world's plan. The world's way is *doing*, God's way is *being made*. To obey God we must take our hands off our own life and then ask God to do with us just what He wants.

Why are so few of us prepared to do this? The answer is simple—it hurts, it costs, it humbles, it denies self—it is not "natural." If we want to bear, however, we should be ready to step aside and let the Lord Jesus, who lives in us by the power of His Holy Spirit, take over the doing and the making and the being.

It costs to be a committed Christian. If I honestly take my hands off my life and say, "Lord, make me what You will," I am opening the door to possible disturbance and difficulty.

If you are a parent, God may want your child for the mission field. If you are younger *your* ambitions may have to go.

God took everything when Nate Saint and his companions prayed this prayer. They had committed all to Him, and there were no strings left for them to pull. But God had a magnificent plan whereby He shocked the Christian world out of its lethargy. Certainly there will be a great Auca harvest, and more certainly there will be a divine, "Well done, thou good and faithful servant!"

Which would you rather do—grow old, fat and prosperous as a "give me" Christian with no real fruit to show. Or live glorious adventure in the uncertainty of *being made* by God losing *things,* and realizing no *reputation,* being a "Fool for Christ's sake."

Emotionally, every one of us would say: "Me for Christ"– but the thing wants considering in the cold light of the cost. Many will say it, but few will take the first step of "nothingness" for Christ's sake, to follow Christ's example and to obey the command: "Let this mind be in you."

When I was staying at the Firs Conference Center in Bellingham, Washington, I was intrigued by the sunlight each morning. Through the windows I saw shadows cast on the road as the sun shone through the tangled mass of fir tree branches. As I studied these patches of sunlight scattered on the road, I suddenly saw something I had learned at school. Among all the varied shapes were a few perfect circles. If the sun is allowed to shine through a hole, whatever shape the hole may be, as long as it is a "nothing" with a complete circumference, the image cast by the sun is always a perfect replica of the shape of the sun, that is, a perfect circle.

76

As I looked I remembered the words of our text: "He made himself nothing." . . . "Let this mind be in you." If I am prepared to make myself nothing, to empty myself, then He, shining through me, can reproduce Himself in this dark world below.

The question is "Dare you so hand over your life to Christ that, as you make yourself nothing, He may move into your entire being to make you according to His own plan and desire?"

The main difficulty in this study is the simplicity of the thought. In our busy world today we are apt to dismiss a thing as trivial, if there is a very simple explanation to it.

We are impressed by the achievements of the "Rocketeers" and the others who put things in orbit, while we take for granted many of the simpler precious achievements of other men.

Philippians 2:7 is divine simplicity, but too many of us are like Naaman, the military leper who at first refused to make himself of nothing by bathing in the poor waters of Jordan. We still cry—"Are not Abana and Pharpar, rivers of Damascus, better than all the waters of Israel?" (II Kings 5:12).

We fail to remember that it was only when Naaman made himself of no reputation, that God *made him* clean!

The world's idea of success is not God's idea. At the end of three years' perfect ministry the Lord Jesus had but twelve apostles, one of whom betrayed Him, one who denied Him, and all forsook Him. From the world's point of view He was a failure, but He could say: "I do always those things that please him" (John 8:29).

He had made the great stoop, had made Himself nothing so that God could take and make Him. His perfect obedience was the answer to it all.

It may come as a shock to some of us that Philippians 2:5 is not a request, it is God's command: "Let this mind be in you, which was also in Christ Jesus."

In other words, if we don't do this then we are disobeying God. The surrounding materialism is such a burden and a barrier. It is so easy to follow the pattern of

77

other much admired Christians and go their way, letting their mind be in us instead of following the mind of Christ. We use this so often as an excuse for not making ourselves of nothing, avoiding thereby the cost, and the shame, and the ridicule.

We should call to mind the names of many missionaries, and servants of God who "made" themselves of no reputation, so that God could move into their lives and use them as He willed.

Like Paul they so often went down in the world's estimation yet they had a greater joy in their nothingness than others had with their possessions.

But God is still no man's debtor. The more you have given, the more God is sure to bless you, even if only to maintain His glorious promises.

"MAKING"

"All things were made by Him," we read.
Without Him nothing can succeed.
And then we read the awful claim,
He made Himself a thing of shame.

He made Himself, and then "was made,"
What agony is here conveyed.
That He, whose power was ever true
Was made, was made for me and you.

Was made a homeless babe to lie,
Was made a homeless passer-by,
That He who gave each bird its nest
Could say—nowhere His head could rest.

His Word says He was made a song
By those the drunken and the wrong.
That His dear eyes were made to cry
For those who saw a loved one die.

It says they made Him bear His cross.
His cross—our joy and hope—His loss,
And then they made Him hang in shame,
They made Him and despised His name.

What wondrous love is here displayed—
"He made Himself—and then was made,"
There was no other way, I know,
They made Him unto death to go.

Lord, teach me now this lesson true,
The truth revealed, displayed thro' you,
That if I would full blessing know,
Then I must also that way go.

I, too, must make myself of naught.
Then—must be made by Thee and taught
That not my way nor thoughts must be
But what Thou, Lord, wilt make of me.

John E. Hunter

CHAPTER 11

THE PRACTICE OF SERVICE

"As they did eat, Jesus took bread, and blessed, and
brake it, and gave to them, and said, Take, eat: this
is my body" (Mark 14:22).

In the last chapter we thought of the principle of
service–not doing, but being made. Now we will see that
God wants not only talented men and women, and those
with special gifts, but the ordinary men and women–
those who are only "five barley loaves and two small
fishes."

One morning in London, I witnessed an unusual sight.
It was rush hour at a busy junction of several roads. The
traffic light had failed and in a very short time every high-
way was snarled up as every driver tried his best to do
his own will. Tension grew.

Suddenly a London policeman appeared. Quickly he
surveyed the scene, and then, walking into the chaos,
took charge. Gradually the blockage eased and soon the
lights began functioning again. The crossing returned to
its usual order.

Because the policeman knew what he was going to do,
he could take charge. This knowledge was the answer to
the problem. This sense of someone in control is a comfort–tempers ease, bitterness disappears, and cooperation
appears.

The "Feeding of the Five Thousand" was something
like that, a build-up of tension and then the sure solution,
because Christ knew what to do.

The story as told in John 6:1-15 would make a wonderful crowd scene for a film. The place was up in the mountains, where it was cool. There was lovely green grass there. Crowds were gathering and building up. John estimates 5,000 men, not counting women and children. There was healing and teaching, the tension was mounting moment by moment. Then it was time to eat. There were no stores, no catering firm had been consulted. Something needed to be done urgently. We can almost see the Lord looking over the great company when He says to Philip: "Where can we buy bread that these may eat?" (John 6:5).

Philip doesn't bother with the where. He simply dismisses the whole thing: "Two hundred pennyworth of bread wouldn't be enough to give them a bite each!" (Remember one penny was a day's wages for a man, so Philip was estimating that it would need nearly a year's wages to give them each a bite.)

Andrew looks around and sees a boy with his lunch– *five barley loaves and two small fishes*–he looks and laughs. He tells the Lord what he can see, and how useless that was.

Philip thought of the financial situation, Andrew of the food situation, and the result was utterly hopeless. But all the time the Lord had worn His calm, confident smile for we read in verse 6: "He himself knew what he would do."

He was master of the situation on the mountain. He asked His question "Where" to test Philip, for all the time the "where" was sitting alongside them in the presence of a small boy. The Lord was not waiting for the money, He was waiting for the boy!

The key to the whole situation is in the words of Andrew in verse 9: "There is a lad here . . ." He was just a very ordinary boy who had tramped the mountains all day, and who was about to devour his tiny lunch. A few hungry bites and it would have vanished. But this lad had something to give, and he was willing to give it to Jesus. Not only had the Lord seen the boy, but the boy had had his eyes fixed on the wonderful teacher. He must have been greatly attracted to the Lord, because he was willing to hand over his lunch in spite of his hunger.

But the most important point is that he really did hand over his precious food to Andrew, who in turn passed it to the Lord.

Many people can *feel* willing to commit their lives to Jesus, their emotions can be aroused, especially in a missionary meeting, tears can flow, and willingness is very evident– but when it comes to the actual handing over then it is quite another story.

What followed next was the wonderful miracle with which we are so familiar. See, first, that it produced complete satisfaction. All those thousands were filled, and not with just a bite as Philip had thought, but a real "all-day-long-mountain-air" hunger was satisfied.

The disciples were satisfied, and so was the Lord–that is a lovely thought–the boy's willingness to give satisfied the hunger of the Son of God. And, of course, the boy was filled. If he had eaten the original it would have left him longing for more, but now he, too, was filled.

Another result of this miracle was an immediate united action on the part of the crowds. They were determined to make Him a king, by force if necessary.

This was one of the high points of our Lord's popularity. The glory, the honor, the united enthusiasm were touched off by a boy's willingness to hand over his little "all."

An examination of the other accounts reveals this sequence of events: The boy handed over his lunch. The Lord took it, He blessed it, He broke it. Then he gave it out to His disciples to distribute among the people. Before the sequence begins there is one boy with his tiny lunch and when it is complete there are thousands of people–fed, and rejoicing. What a wonderful teaching this is!

Let us apply this lesson to our own lives. Around us is a world weary, broken and hungry. Even thousands of people today in this prosperous land are hungry–hungry for some means of satisfying the inner longings in their hearts.

The human heart needs more than cars, T.V. sets, and new houses to meet its inner hunger. The rich and prosperous are just as hungry as the down-and-outs, so are the famous and the religious.

For today's crowd, also, Jesus says: "Where shall we buy bread that these may eat?" The Lord is not looking for money, He is waiting for the boy, for us, to give all that we possess.

Humanly speaking, all the honor the Lord received that day came because there was a boy who had something to give, and he gave it willingly. Are you willing to do the same?

"Oh," you reply, "I can't preach or sing–or play or anything–I'm no use!" In other words you are just "five barley loaves and two small fishes"–the most ordinary things you could find. But realize that it was with the ordinary that the Lord did the extra-ordinary. Your life, however drab and ordinary it seems to you is still barley loaves and fishes!

The lad was willing to give what he had, because of love to Christ. Do you love Him enough to give him your barley loaves and fishes as a love gift?

Being willing, emotionally, it not enough. There must be the one act of decision when we hand over into the hands of the Lord we love, all that we have and are. Commitment to Christ is the spark that can fire a great sequence of miracles. For we commit to Him our all and He takes it.

Christ blessed the food. Just as surely, if we yield to Him ourselves, He will hold us in His hands and bless us. After He took, He blessed, then–after He blessed it, He brake it. The gift was broken up into small pieces.

Sometimes this is what the Lord does with us, too; He breaks us. At times we find ourselves in sorrow or loss. Things go wrong for no apparent reason. We are tempted to cry, "Why should God do this to me?"

He may be breaking the bread with which to feed others.

> . . . . the God of all comfort; Who comforteth us in all our tribulation, that we may be able to comfort them which are in any trouble, by the comfort wherewith we ourselves are comforted of God (II Corinthians 1:3, 4).

Notice two things.

First, the breaking was done in His own hands. Our troubles and distresses are not suffered out of the hands of Christ but safely in His hands.

> My sheep hear my voice, and I know them, and they follow me: And I give unto them eternal life; and they shall never perish, neither shall any man pluck them out of my hand. My Father, which gave them me, is greater than all; and no man is able to pluck them out of my Father's hand. I and my Father are one (John 10:27–30).

Surely as Jesus said: "neither shall any pluck them out of my hand"–He would hold one cupped hand, and as He said–"no man is able to pluck them out of my Father's hand"; He would hold up the other cupped hand. But how can we be in two hands at once?

"I and My Father are one" is the answer. Jesus would bring His two hands together to make one place of shelter, and right in the center of the two hands is where we can rest.

Second, the thing to realize in connection with this idea of "breaking," is that the Lord always fed people with broken bread. Mark 14:22 says: "And as they did eat, Jesus took bread, and blessed, and brake it, and gave to them, and said, Take, eat: this is my body."

Notice the same order again, He took–blessed–brake–gave.

Luke 24:30 says: "And it came to pass, as he sat at meat with them, he took bread, and blessed it, and brake, and gave to them." The same order again. Notice, especially, the beginning of verse 31: "And their eyes were opened, and they knew him." They recognized the broken bread–in the broken hands.

The most precious thing ever to be broken was the precious body of Christ.

This thought of Christ feeding people on broken bread is so vital in our service. In the last chapter we had the simple thought that first–*He made himself* and then *He was made*–this being the divine principle of all service, ours included.

If we then, having made ourselves of nothing, hand over our whole being to Him–we shall "be made." That was the principle, now here is the practice of the principle. We are to be in His hands with no reserve of any kind, and in the hands the breaking is done.

Notice that many of us need breaking because we are too big or too hard–Christ's standard size is "a grain of wheat!"

The need for "breaking" may be very real. There may be friendships that will need breaking, if Christ is to have all of me to "make me" as He desires. Sometimes it is our friendships with other people that drag us down, or pull us away.

If the rocket is to rise it must sever all connection with the world around it so that it can soar unhindered.

Habits, too, may need breaking. Habits that are suitable for a worldling but which dishonor Christ. Here, again, learn the lesson that we do not have to break the friendship or break the habit. If we stay in His hands, He will do the breaking.

I remember one young man who had just been gloriously saved asking how he could break with all his old friends and acquaintances. He knew he would have to finish with them, but he wondered how to break with them. The answer was simple. He was told simply to let the Lord Jesus take his life to do with as He chose, and the problem would solve itself. His friends would go of their own accord. As they saw his habits being broken by Christ, so the friendship would either be broken or united in Christ.

Christ, too, can give us a break with past failure. II Corinthians 5:17 says: "Therefore if any man be in Christ, he is a new creature: old things are passed away; behold, all things are become new." The chains that bind us with the past, with others and with ourselves, can be broken–in His hands.

The whole situation in this story is so human–the build up of a difficult situation so common in life today–the emphasis on the financial and the material side–when, all the time the answer is there in the midst. How very often a church, or a group, can be searching for a way out of a difficulty, trying the usual financial ways, or the obvious material ways, wondering what on earth to do, when, all the time the answer is in their midst.

The boy had no idea what the Lord would do with his loaves and fishes. Undoubtedly he was offering to Christ in love–for Christ to eat–not the crowd.

When the call comes to give, let us do it unto the Lord. What He does with the gift is His business, not ours.

Christ said in I Corinthians 11:24:

This is my body, which is broken for you.

Psalm 51:17 says:

The sacrifices of God are a broken spirit: a broken and a contrite heart, O God, thou wilt not despise.

God does not ask for our money or our talents, He asks: "My Son, give me thine heart" (Proverbs 23:26). Romans 12:1 calls us to present our bodies unto God–to hand over ourselves, all that we are. We are the five barley loaves and the two small fishes.

I beseech you therefore, brethren, by the mercies of God, that ye present your bodies a living sacrifice, holy, acceptable unto God, which is your reasonable service (Romans 12:1).

CHAPTER 12

LORDSHIP IN SERVICE

"Then Jesus said to them again, Peace be unto you: as my Father hath sent me, even so send I you" (John 20:21).

We use the term the Lord Jesus Christ, but so often we treat the word "Lord" as a term of affection, not as a title. If we could only realize Who He is, and recognize His authority in our lives, half of the worries and problems that beset us would vanish. Many of these problems are caused by two-faced Christian living. Trying to serve two masters, instead of owning one Lord.

Statistics generally accepted for the world wastage-rate on Christian mission fields overseas, show some searching facts. First they tell us that out of all the men and women who go to a foreign field, only about half return after the first period of service, some are back before the first period is finished.

Secondly they say that after ten years only ten per cent are still on the field. We realize, of course, that for some, the reason for not returning is the twin problem of health and home. But, when there is so much eagerness to go out first of all, and such an obvious point of weakness in the going out again, might it not be that some who went should not have gone at the first. Could it be over-enthusiasm, emotional reaction to a challenge given?

We want to face this problem in the light of the sovereignty of Christ.

The full title of Christ is: "Our Lord and Saviour Jesus

Christ." Notice the order of the words—He is not only our *Saviour* but *Our Lord and Saviour*.

Much gospel preaching dwells on Jesus as our Saviour, but almost ignores the first title—"Lord." Unfortunately, dwelling on "Saviour" emphasizes what we get out of the work of Christ. If we use the word "Lord," the emphasis is on what we must give *Him*. To leave out the Lordship is to be selfish, because it means that we want the riches without the responsibility.

Christianity is not a democracy, it is a dictatorship— and that is where many of us go wrong. We do not believe in lords and kings in America—we have elected representatives. We pretend it is so in our spiritual lives. If we do not agree with the Lord, we elect representatives— usually ourself!

But the whole structure of our faith in God is built on the words of Christ in Mark 12:29, 30: "The Lord our God is one Lord: and thou shalt love the Lord thy God with all thy heart, and with all thy soul, and with all thy mind, and with all thy strength." Remember, too, that Christ said in John 14:15: "If ye love Me, keep My commandments."

If He is my Lord then I am His slave to command. It is my responsibility to run at His ordering. The slave never questions an order given, he had no right to—he had no rights at all. His lord held the right, the reason, the responsibility; the slave had only to produce the results. Is Jesus Christ our Lord in this way?

With this thought in mind let us look at John 20:21: ". . . as my Father hath sent me, even so send I you." Now see this same thought in John 17:18: "As thou hast sent me into the world, even so have I also sent them into the world." This is the act of our Lord—He sends. This is, once again, one of the simple truths in the word we so often overlook. Just as in Philippians 2:7 we do not "do," we "are made," so here we do not "go," we "are sent."

This is the real basis of our responsibility in service— not to go here, or go there, as we feel there is a need, but to go as we are sent. Sometimes we are so busy "going" that we are not available to be "sent." Even service on the mission field has the same basis. We do not *go* simply because we are sorry for the poor heathen; we go because we are *sent*.

Isaiah responded the correct way. "Also I heard the voice of the Lord, saying, Whom shall I send, and who will go for us? Then said I, Here am I: send me" (Isaiah 6:8).

Let us think of the idea of being sent: "As thou hast sent me into the world, even so have I also also sent them into the world" (John 17:18).

Just as He was sent by the Father, He says we are to be sent. Notice—Jesus did not "go," He "was sent."

1. *Sent for the Same Purpose*

We also share the purpose for which Christ was sent. If we can find His purpose, we can know our purpose. The answer is given in John 17:4: "I have glorified thee on the earth. . . ."

The main purpose Christ had on earth was to glorify the Father. Saving sinners was a sub-heading under glorifying. The Westminster Catechism is relevant again:

"What is the chief end of man?"

"Man's chief end is to glorify God and to enjoy Him for ever."

Many Christians think that their chief aim in Christian service is to win souls, to preach the gospel, to get on with the job. This sounds very natural. But our Lord sends us first of all, to glorify God. Not to quit our jobs and rush off to the mission field—our first purpose is to glorify God. See how comforting this is to a faithful soul. There can be a lot of glamor in being a missionary—I know because I am one—we have given up so much for the Lord, etc. etc., and we come in for such a lot of praise and hero-worship.

Someone said to me recently, "Oh, I think you are wonderful, you've given up such a good job, with such excellent prospects, all for God!" Nonsense, I didn't give it up—I was sent, I can do no other!

Often God is more glorified in the quiet, witness of a busy mother living to the glory of God in a needy neighborhood, or a workman or storekeeper, glorifying God by a radiant faith that shines in the place of other people's failures and defeats. Yes, we are sent first of all to glorify God.

How did Christ glorify His Father? The answer is in the other half of verse 4: "I have finished the work which thou gavest me to do." He glorified God by finishing the work which He was given to do. The work was not something He thought up—He was given the work to do, and He finished it!

What a challenge is there for us—finishing a task we never chose. One of the weaknesses of our churches today are the Christians who get bright ideas to start a job, but when it gets too irksome they drop it and start something else. We meet them everywhere, Christians rushing around first to one thing then to another. It all looks so busy. Jesus said: "I have finished the work which Thou gavest me to do." What a difference.

Christ glorified His Father in another way. John 8:29 says: "I do always those things that please him." (The One that sent Him.) Always, all those things that please Him. Check this with the last verse in John's gospel:

There are also many other things which Jesus did, the which, if they should be written every one, I suppose that even the world itself could not contain the books that should be written.

Many other things—always those things that please the Father.

Christ glorified the Father in His unfaltering obedience —always, in all things. (Luke 2:52 and Luke 3:22). We can truthfully say that the measure of glory we yield to God is the measure of obedience we return to Him. This is shown most solemnly by the Lord in Matthew 7:21:

"Not every one that saith unto me, Lord, Lord, shall enter into the kingdom of heaven; but he that doeth the will of my Father which is in heaven."

Response to Lordship is tested not by the works done, but by the obedience given. In Matthew 7:22 those who profess to call Him Lord tell of the many wonderful works which they have done, but Christ refuses to own them. Religious activity is no substitute for obedience to God.

These two thoughts of finishing the unchosen task, and doing it in complete obedience, are beautifully illustrated for us in the last recorded letter of Paul: "I have fought a good fight, I have finished my course, I have kept the faith" (II Timothy 4:7). He finished his course in full and faithful obedience.

2. *In the Same Manner*

Even so have I also sent them–in the same manner. In what manner was Christ sent by the Father? When we learn that, we can then apply it to our own hearts.

An examination of John 6 from verses 35 to the end of the chapter shows the gradual buildup of opposition to Christ.

Compare the thoughts of verse 41–"The Jews then murmured . . ." and verse 52: "The Jews therefore strove among themselves . . ." with verse 61: "his disciples murmured . . ." and verse 66: "From that time many of his disciples went back, and walked no more with him." The disciples were infected by the complaint of the Jews— why? Verses 56 and 57 caused the breakdown–"He that eateth my flesh, and drinketh my blood, dwelleth in me and I in him. As the living Father hath sent me, and I live by the Father: so he that eateth me, even he shall live by me."

The Amplified Bible brings out the reaction of the disciples to this truth–verse 60: "When His disciples heard this, many of them said, This is a hard and difficult and strange saying–an offensive and unbearable message. Who can stand to hear it?–Who can be expected to listen to such teaching?"

The reason for this breakdown in relationships was that the Lord brought in the new challenge that hurt them. These disciples didn't mind being with the Lord when there was all the excitement of the healings, and the miracles, and the feeding of the 5,000.

They didn't mind being occupied in seeing all the sights–but now the Lord was teaching that "occupation" wasn't enough. His new call was to "identification" and not "occupation." Verse 57 makes this so clear: "As the living Father hath sent me, and I live by the Father. . . ." The same "as" and "so" message–"Just as the living Father hath sent me and I live by, or through, the Father– so he that eateth me, even he shall live by me, even so, in just the same way, whoever continues to feed on me shall live through me." The link that united the Father to the Son has to be that by which we are united to Him. We have to continue to feed on Him, the ultimate form of identification. We become what we eat–if I eat poor food my physical health will suffer, if I eat infected food I will be ill, if I eat poisoned food I will die. Jesus says we have to feed on Him.

I remember once seeing a Moody Science film which showed how very quickly the food we ate traveled along the blood stream to the extremities of the fingers. Food eaten and passed into the blood stream was proved to be reaching all over the body in a matter of seconds.

If I feed on Christ and continue to feed on Him it will affect every part of my being–my mind with its thoughts, ambitions, associations; my emotions with the quickly responsive reactions; my will, when infilled with the living Christ, will be alive to do His will.

The living Christ will bring the tingle of life to all my personality, a pure, holy, godly life. All this is in the present tense–we continue to feed on Him. He continues to live in us and that is how He sends us–*Even so send I you*–in the same manner, identified with Christ in every part of my being.

This again to us is the challenge, this is where it hurts. We don't mind having a church life in which we are fully occupied with committees, groups, activities, choirs, societies, etc., but when the Lord, your Lord, my Lord, calls us, not to a church life with its happy, respectable activities, but to be identified with Him in what may prove to be loneliness, despising and forsaking, then verse 66 comes true again, and many of His disciples still go back and walk no more with Him. Occupation—yes; identification—no.

This does not mean that I become a kill-joy—no, for the joy of the Lord fills my heart. But it does mean that I must be "not of the world" as He was "not of the world." "Remember the word that I said unto you, The servant is not greater than his Lord. If they have persecuted me, they will also persecute you; if they have kept my sayings, they will keep yours also" (John 15:20). See once again the Lord talking to His servant, your Lord talking to you.

The whole of the Old Testament is a repeated presentation of the fact that "The Lord, he is the God; the Lord, he is the God" (I Kings 18:39). When God's people recognized this fact and humbled themselves then they prospered.

"That at the name of Jesus every knee should bow . . . and that every tongue should confess that Jesus Christ is Lord, to the glory of God the Father" (Philippians 2:10, 11).

Notice this stipulates every knee, not only the heathen but the Christians too. He is Lord of all.

This is good old-fashioned theology which is often forgotten in these modern days. God is still the same, His attributes are still the same. Revelation 4:11 is an everlasting truth: "Thou art worthy, O Lord, to receive glory and honor and power: for thou hast created all things, and for thy pleasure they are and were created." Press home to your heart the truth that my first aim is to glorify God. Challenge yourself on this point, asking, Does my life glorify God even *now*? Do my dress, my habits, my friends, my speech, and the books I read glorify God?

93

This is one of the most humbling and challenging thoughts in the Word of God. To use a military term "Operation Glory is priority number one." Failure on this point, to glorify God, means failure to the words—*Even so, send I you.*

This is the challenge that weeded out the disciples. The "Good time" followers soon broke away when the call to identification came.

"So send I you. . ."

CHAPTER 13

NOTHINGNESS IN SERVICE

"Then answered Jesus and said unto them, Verily, verily, I say unto you, The Son can do nothing of himself, but what he seeth the Father do: for what things soever he doeth, these also doeth the Son likewise" (John 5:19).

Notice what an amazing statement this is—*The Son can do nothing of Himself*. The deeds He performed were done because of, and through the One, Who sent Him. And the Lord says—*even so send I you* (John 20: 21). We can apply this to ourselves—we can do nothing of ourselves, any deeds of true service for God will be performed by the One Who sent us. Notice how definite this teaching is, it takes *us* right out of the picture.

If any *real* service is to be done then it must be done by the One Who sends me. Christ living in me, in the person of His Holy Spirit, must be able to use me as the vehicle or implement of His divine will.

It is my responsibility to say "Yes Lord, here I am, send me and use me." All Christ wants of me is my availability.

So I don't go—I am sent, and when I am sent I don't initiate the doing, I simply present myself to be used by the one who sent me.

Someone might say, "Isn't that a dangerous idea, after all if I don't get on with the job nothing will be done!" Yet Jesus said, if *you do* get on with the job then nothing will be done—you can do nothing of true value for God apart from the inward working of Christ.

95

Always remember that running here and there, being on this committee and this group, etc. etc., does not necessarily mean that it is true productive service for God. No one *sees* the trees growing or the flowers opening, but they do grow and open. There is no noise or excitement as the stars and planets move on their courses but they do. We can never imagine the Lord in a rush or a panic, but "all things were accomplished."

"I can of mine own self do nothing: as I hear, I judge: and my judgment is just; because I seek not mine own will, but the will of the Father which hath sent me" (John 5:30). Here is the same thought again. His decisions were not His own. How terribly this fact is illustrated in Matthew 26:39–"O my Father, if it be possible, let this cup pass from me: nevertheless, not as I will, but as thou wilt." The desire was His, in all His humanity but the decision was the will of the One who sent Him. And Our Lord says to us–"Even so send I you."

We, too, may have human desires but the decision must not be ours but from Him that sent us. Remember, our main thought is the Lordship of Christ–the Lord and the slave–we have no decisions. We must be ready to do as Mary said in John 2:5 "Whatsoever he saith unto you, do it!" She was able to say that because she began her service for God by saying–"Behold the handmaid of the Lord; be it unto me according to thy word." If this is our attitude to our Lord then many of the problems of life will be settled for us because our own desires, however good and sincere, will not be the deciding factor. The decision will be in relation to the fact that we are sent.

If my Lord is sending me for a certain job He will also supply all that I need–"But my God shall supply all your need according to his riches in glory by Christ Jesus" (Philippians 4:19).

Regarding this verse, Charles Haddon Spurgeon, the great English preacher of the last generation, used to say it was God's check. The company was "My God." The

96

promise on the check was "shall supply." The amount written was "all your need." The account was "His riches." The bank was "in glory" and the signature on the check was "By Jesus Christ."

Again we are faced with the fact that so many Christians have never proved God. They have never taken Him at His word and launched out on His promise. This is why we are continually called to—"rest in the Lord—commit thy way unto the Lord." Let the decisions be His, for Christ said—"Even so send I you."

"Jesus answered them, and said, my doctrine is not mine, but his that sent me" (John 7:16).

Many in the world today accept Christ not as the Saviour but as a great teacher. This is a remarkable fact for in several places our Lord disclaimed all responsibility for His teaching. As in this verse, He teaches that He has no doctrine, no ideas or views of His own. All the pronouncements from His lips came from the One Who sent Him. He gave all the authority and the glory to God—"Even so send I you"—under the same conditions.

Just as the Lord constantly hid Himself behind the One Who sent Him, seeking no privileges, expecting no rights because He was the sent one—"even so send I you."

We must learn to let the Word of God be the answer to the many questions that crop up. We must stop quoting our views and airing our opinions and remember always—"My doctrine is not Mine but His that sent me."

Let us remember that when Christ faced the tempter in the wilderness He never used any new ideas or techniques, He quoted from the Word of God. Whether in defence, or decree, His doctrine wasn't His own. The Word of God is sufficient for you and for me.

"For I have not spoken of myself; but the Father which sent me, he gave me a commandment, what I should say, and what I should speak." (John 12:49).

It is amazing how, as we read John's gospel, we meet the same idea over and over again—"Not mine but the

Father which sent me." The recurrence of the phrase is surely not accidental.

The Lord constantly effaced Himself and always brought in "the Father which hath sent Me." Here He teaches that He had been given orders what to say. The authority of God was behind His words. Just as of old the prophets cried—"Thus saith the Lord"—and pronounced the message God had given them, so Christ spoke. His words carried weight, there was a crispness of authority so that men said—"Never man spake like this man" (John 7:46). But He was only being faithful to Him Who sent Him—"Even so send I you."

We who teach and preach and guide in the things of God are sent not to speak of ourselves but—"the Saviour, which sent me. He gave commandment what I should say, and what I should speak." Popularity in preaching is not always a sign of faithfulness in preaching.

Paul, writing in II Corinthians 5:20 gives an excellent illustration of the idea: "Now then we are ambassadors for Christ, as though God did beseech you by us: we pray you in Christ's stead, be ye reconciled to God." His message is—"be ye reconciled to God," but God is doing the beseeching through Paul, and Christ is doing the speaking through Paul. Paul is simply the vehicle of the Godhead.

He was an ambassador. Notice that an ambassador is always sent, he never goes where he chooses. When he arrives, he, himself, is 'a nothing,' but he represents everything. When the American Ambassador in Paris speaks—America is speaking. He doesn't say what he likes if he is a faithful ambassador, he speaks the words of the one who sent him. The Amabassador is not ashamed to witness for his country. His residence flies the flag of America, his automobile displays the flag—he is America.

Therefore his conduct has to honor his country, and he has to be guarded in his speech. He is the chosen vessel sent to a foreign land, he is the mouthpiece of his country.

In like manner, we, too, are ambassadors for Christ, we are to be faithful, unashamed, displaying our flag, and the words we speak are the words of our Lord— "Even so send I you."

CHAPTER 14

GOD'S RULES FOR SERVICE

"Now all these things happened unto them for en-
samples: and they are written for our admonition, upon
whom the ends of the world are come" (I Corinthians
10:11).

The Israelites limited what God could do *for* them,
because of their selfishness and their lack of faith. It
wasn't that God wasn't powerful enough but that the
Almighty, omnipotent God was limited by the creatures
He had redeemed. God could have done so much more
for them. It wasn't God's idea to wander in a desert, He
had Canaan all ready but they refused to enter in.

Truly this is a type of many of God's people today. We
have been redeemed from bondage, redeemed by the
blood of the Lamb, but, like the Israelites, so many wander in a desert of their own choosing.

They wander and limit God, limit all that He could do
for them in the way of peace, comfort, assurance and
confidence in Christ. The wilderness was a place of
murmurings and mistakes. So often they were rebellious
(just as we are), and God had to chasten them. So many
of God's people are in a desert of their own making. They
murmur and cry, "Why should God do this to me?" yet
so often it is not what God has done, but what they have
chosen. If I put my finger into a fire I must not blame
God if I get burned!

The wilderness was a place of fruitlessness. They were
constantly looking back to Egypt and thinking of the
"pleasures" of Egypt–they had refused to enter the land

flowing with milk and honey. It was not God's plan that they should wander in a fruitless place.

A wilderness experience in the Christian life can be just as fruitless, just as unsatisfying.

Many of God's people have nothing to show for years of being on the Christian pathway. Many churches are composed of groups of wilderness Christians so that the witness of the church is fruitless, joyless and dead.

Limiting God in what He can do for us is bad enough, but then there is the other side which is so much worse. We limit God in what He can do through us. When God called us to Himself, and cleansed us from our sins, and gave us the gift of eternal life it was for a definite purpose: "Yield yourselves unto God, as those that are alive from the dead, and your members as instruments of righteousness unto God" (Romans 6:13). The Amplified Bible uses the phrase "implements of righteousness."

We are saved for a very definite purpose–that we, our whole, entire selves, might be instruments, or weapons, or implements, in the hand of God.

Now, think how much we must hinder what God can do through us. All true Christians are the means whereby God fulfills His purpose, fights His battles and feeds the spiritually hungry. Weakness and failure on our part lead to God being limited in what He can do through us.

Perhaps God wants to do a mighty work in your school, in your store, in your church, in your family or whatever it may be, but He cannot, because you are fearful, in spite of all His promises. "Greater is he that is in you than he that is in the world" (I John 4:4).

You and I are wonderfully equipped, we are invincibly strong, because Christ lives in us in the power of His Holy Spirit. But in spite of this we still limit what God can do through us. We are useless instruments, idle implements, and frightened weapons.

If every Christian was available to God and served Him as fearlessly as the Communists serve their masters, what a different story there would be. A true Communist considers himself expendable for the cause, no sacrifice is too great to ask, or too difficult to perform. No wonder the power of communism is spreading, they never turn back, no matter how great the problems.

Often, too, we hinder God's work through sheer selfishness. Remember that God doesn't want our money, or our support, or our patronage—He wants *you*.—"Yield yourselves . . . and your members." All that you are and all that you have. Many Christians think this is carrying things a bit too far. "To hand over your whole life to Christ! That's a bit too much! You must be reasonable in all things!"

Through our sheer selfishness we hinder God: "The godly man ceaseth . . . the faithful fail" (Psalm 12:1). Why do they cease and fail? Verse 4 has the answer: "Our lips are our own: who is Lord over us?"

This is true today in our churches. People who once were godly are ceasing, and those who once were faithful are failing.

The reason is the same—sheer selfishness. They say— "My time is my own! Who is going to tell me what I have to do?"

I have a glorious inheritance in Christ. "In whom also we have obtained an inheritance" (Ephesians 1:11). He is the source of all my cleansing, my comfort and my joy. How gladly we go to our Lord Jesus and tell Him our sorrows and expect Him to comfort us. How willingly He meets all our need. He, Himself, is our rich inheritance. But look at verse 18 of the same chapter: "His inheritance in the saints." It works both ways. I am His inheritance, all that He needs He should be able to find in me. But we are selfish—we say to God, "Give, give, give and forgive!" But our own personal relationship is "Get, get, get—and forget!" Thus we hinder God's work in all the many wonderful things He could do through us. "Wherefore let him that thinketh he standeth take heed lest he fall" (I Corinthians 10:12).

In God's dealings with His people He gave them many warnings, but eventually the end came. II Chronicles 36:16 states: "But they mocked the messengers of God, and despised his words, and misused his prophets, until the wrath of the Lord arose against his people, till there was no remedy." How tragic are those last words—"till there was no remedy." We must realize that today we are the messengers sent with a warning.

How much more fruitful could we be if we did not hinder God's work because we go our own way, work out our own plans, and are unwilling to get off the throne of our heart and let Christ have full control.

"Commit thy way unto the Lord; trust also in him; and he shall bring it to pass" (Psalm 37:5).

"And the very God of peace sanctify you wholly; and I pray God your whole spirit and soul and body be preserved blameless unto the coming of our Lord Jesus Christ" (I Thessalonians 5:23). God wants us to enjoy not only what God has done for us, not only His work, but His very Person. *He is our peace—He is our life.* If we can come to the place where we commit all that we are, and hope to be, into His hands—and then rest there, thanking Him for what He has done—not asking Him over and over again to do what He has already done—then we can find peace and enjoy what God has for us.

"But as it is written, Eye hath not seen, nor ear heard, neither have entered into the heart of man, the things which God hath prepared for them that love him. But God hath revealed them unto us by his Spirit" (I Corinthians 2:9, 10). So often verse 9 is quoted by itself as being heaven to come, but verse 10 distinctly says: "But God hath revealed them unto us by his Spirit." All these precious things are ours to enjoy now, as we enter into all that Christ is now.

Living the Christ-filled life is thus a joyous experience of being totally involved with the living victorious Christ. It is the outcome of willing obedience. It is the delight of daily discipline. It is what God intended the Christian life to be. It is yours for the taking, the trusting and the triumphing.